An A to Z

CUMBRIA AND THE LAKE DISTRICT ON FILM

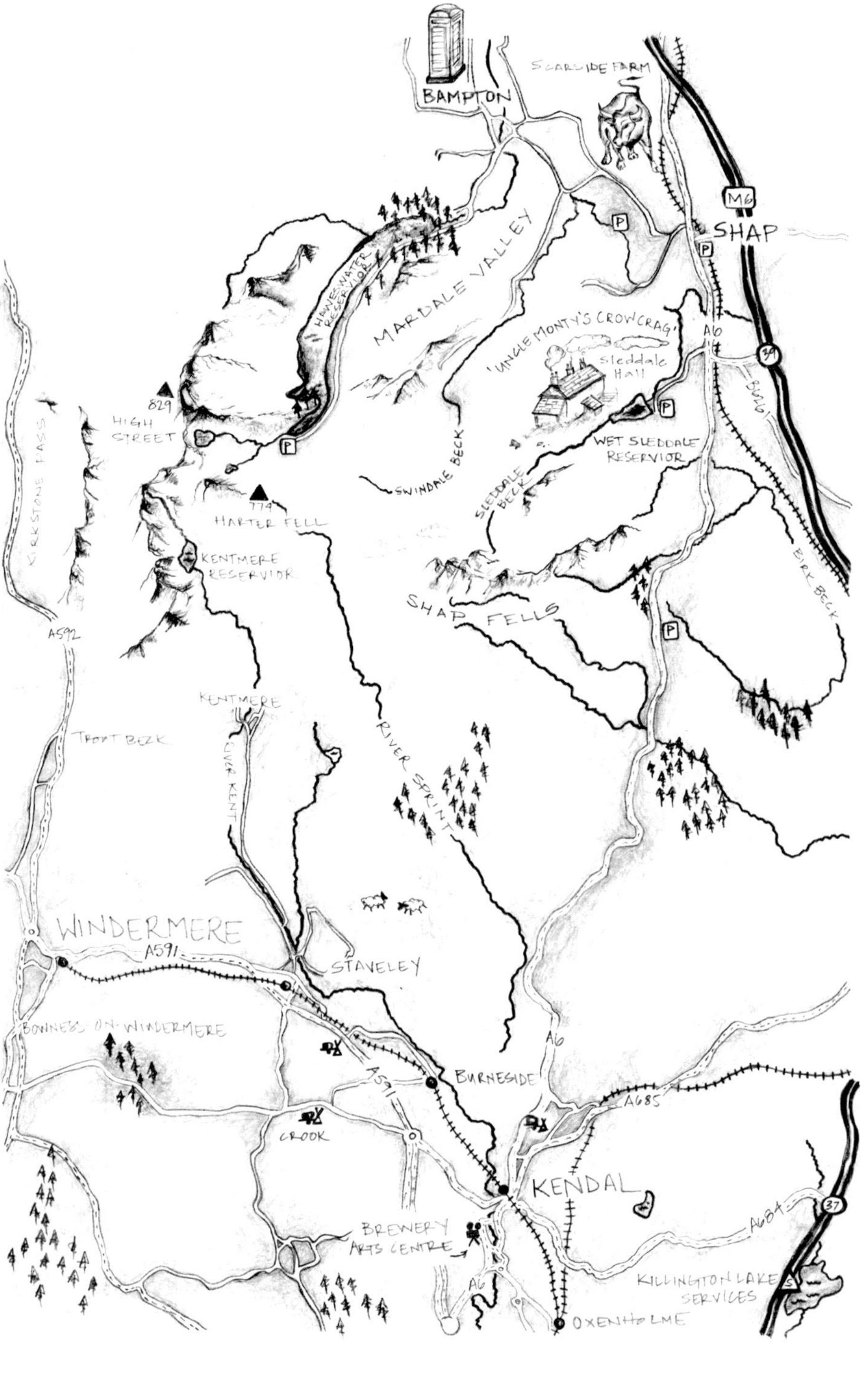

BAMPTON
SCARSIDE FARM
M6
SHAP
HAWESWATER RESERVOIR
MARDALE VALLEY
'UNCLE MONTY'S CROW CRAG'
Sleddale Hall
A6
39
829
HIGH STREET
P
WET SLEDDALE RESERVIOR
SWINDALE BECK
SLEDDALE BECK
774
HARTER FELL
KIRKSTONE PASS
KENTMERE RESERVIOR
SHAP FELLS
BIRK BECK
A592
KENTMERE
TROUT BECK
RIVER KENT
RIVER SPRINT
WINDERMERE
A591
STAVELEY
BOWNESS-ON-WINDERMERE
A6
BURNESIDE
A591
A685
CROOK
KENDAL
37
A684
BREWERY ARTS CENTRE
A6
KILLINGTON LAKE SERVICES
OXENHOLME

A Cumbria Guide

An A to Z

CUMBRIA AND THE LAKE DISTRICT ON FILM

David Banning

with map illustrations by Eileen Pun

HAYLOFT PUBLISHING LTD
CUMBRIA

First published by Hayloft 2016

Hayloft Publishing Ltd, Kendal, Cumbria.

tel: 07971 352473
email: books@hayloft.eu
web: www.hayloft.eu

ISBN 978-1-910237-18-2

Copyright © David Banning, 2016

David Banning has asserted his right to be identified
as the Author of this Work

This book is sold subject to the condition that it shall not, by way of trade or otherwise, be lent, resold, hired out, or otherwise circulated without the publisher's prior consent in any form of binding or cover other than that in which it is published and without a similar condition including this condition being imposed on the subsequent purchaser.

A CIP catalogue record for this book is available
from the British Library

Papers used by Hayloft are natural, recyclable products made from wood grown in sustainable forests. The manufacturing processes conform to the environmental regulations of the country of origin.

Designed, printed and bound in the EU

Jacket image: Paul McGeoch, www.paulmcgeoch.com
and font: Daniel Hochard, Imagex Fonts
Maps: Eileen Pun
Frontispiece: Withnail map.

For Dad, R.I.P.

Map of part of Cumbria showing the sites of the author's top ten films (see page 10).

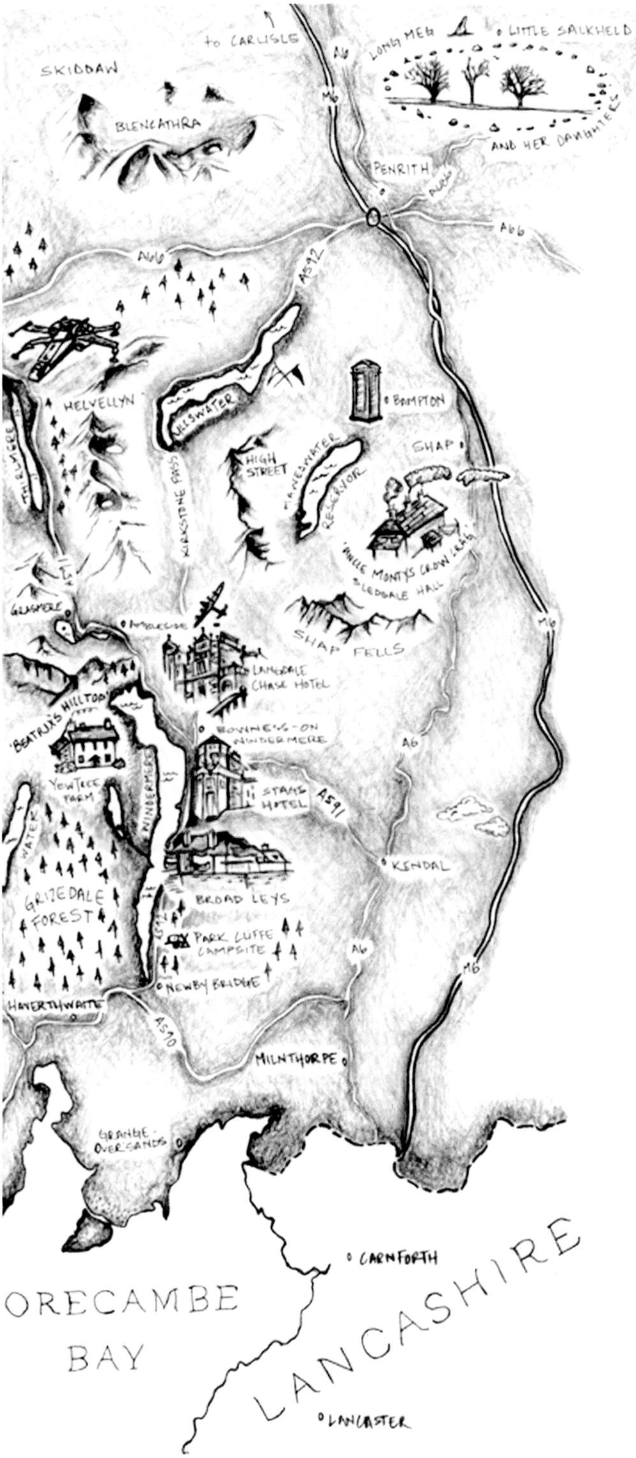

to CARLISLE
SKIDDAW
BLENCATHRA
LONG MEG
LITTLE SALKHELD
AND HER DAUGHTERS
A6
M6
PENRITH
A66
A592
HELVELLYN
ULLSWATER
BAMPTON
SHAP
THIRLMERE
KIRKSTONE PASS
HIGH STREET
HAWESWATER
RESERVOIR
'UNCLE MONTY'S CROW CRAG'
SLEDDALE HALL
SHAP FELLS
LANGDALE CHASE HOTEL
'BEATRIX'S HILLTOP'
BOWNESS-ON WINDERMERE
YEW TREE FARM
WINDERMERE
STAMS HOTEL
A591
KENDAL
GRIZEDALE FOREST
BROAD LEYS
PARK CLIFFE CAMPSITE
NEWBY BRIDGE
HAVERTHWAITE
A590
MILNTHORPE
GRANGE-OVERSANDS
CARNFORTH
MORECAMBE BAY
LANCASHIRE
LANCASTER

An A to Z: Cumbria and the Lake District on Film

Contents

Ten of the Best	10
Foreword by Sophie Neville	11
Introduction	14
Cumbria and the Lake District A-Z of films	19
Selected Cumbrian Cinemas	164
Film Festivals	167
Websites	171
Afterword	174
Acknowledgements	175
Film Index	176
The Author	178

Ten of the Best

Listed in date order with locations:

Brief Encounter, 1945 – Carnforth Station, Lancashire. Middle Fell Bridge, Langdale Beck, Dungeon Ghyll.

The Dambusters, 1955 – Derwentwater, Grasmere Lake, Langdale Chase Hotel: Windermere.

Swallows and Amazons, 1974 – Coniston, Grizedale Forest, Derwentwater, Bowness-on-Windermere, Elterwater, Haverthwaite,

The French Lieutenant's Woman, 1981 – Broad Leys: Windermere.

Brazil, 1985 – Newlands Hause, Newlands Valley.

Withnail & I, 1987 – Crow Crag: Wet Sleddale, Bampton, Tailbert, Keld and Haweswater.

28 Days Later, 2002 – Bowness Knott, Ennerdale Water.

Miss Potter, 2006 – Loughrigg Tarn, Yew Tree Farm, Tarn Hows, Miresyke (overlooking Loweswater), Derwentwater, Whitehaven ('the Rum Story').

Sightseers, 2012 – Keswick Pencil Museum, Honister Pass, Long Meg and Her Daughters stone circle, Park Cliffe campsite, Windermere.

Star Wars Episode VII – The Force Awakens, 2015 – Derwentwater, Thirlmere.

Foreword

I'M often asked, 'What was filming in the Lake District like? Was it fun?' In 1973 I was given the lead part of Titty in the EMI feature film *Swallows and Amazons*, one of the few movies almost entirely shot on location in what is now Cumbria. Although I have since been filming all over the world – from London to the Island of Corfu – I remember working in the Lake District with great affection. We were embraced by north country hospitality and never let down by the hard-working locals who provided vehicles, boats and locations. As Virginia McKenna, cast in the role of my mother said, 'it was one of the happiest times I ever spent on a film.' Being in the fells took us away from our everyday existence and opened our eyes to something greater – including the Lakeland sense of humour.

The film crew were delighted to find a range of accommodation and places to eat in Ambleside. Ronald Fraser, starring in the movie as Captain Flint, soon found all the best pubs in Cumbria. Extracting him became tricky, and who could blame him when his part entailed descending under the surface of Derwent Water?

Our film was set in 1929, a point that caused more problems than the good pubs. We were filming back in 1973, when long hair was all the rage, and couldn't find any men in the Lake District under the age of eighty willing to have a short back-and-sides. They encountered the same obstacle when making the new film adaptation of *Swallows and Amazons* in 2015. Traditional boats were far easier to come by.

Historic buildings abound in Cumbria, but plan ahead if you need interiors. Mrs Batty of Bank Ground Farm, above Coniston Water, was horrified when our art director began adapting her home into the farmhouse remembered by Arthur Ransome as Holly Howe. She locked out the film crew until she received substantial restitution of a financial nature. I don't think she ever knew that Ian Whittaker, the set dresser who'd torn the trendy lino from her kitchen floor in search of authentic Westmorland flagstones, ended up winning two Oscars for set design.

Local people such as Kerry Darbishire and the Price family had small parts in the film, and other Cumbrian characters got involved. Norman Allonby built a traditional charcoal burner's wigwam with a working fireplace so solid that the remains can still be found in the Grizedale Forest today. Mrs Proctor of Kendal provided Captain Flint's green parrot. He was a male bird and had never been on a houseboat before, but took on the speaking role of Polly with some flare. Mrs Dora Capstick of Ambleside taught Ronald Fraser to play the accordion. She did so well that he managed to play 'What Shall We Do With the Drunken Sailor' whilst still a bit tiddly from the Wrap Party two nights before.

We had a fishing scene, shot near the reed banks of Elterwater. Great care was taken of the fish including one playing Roger's shark, a massive pike that we wanted to return to the wild. It developed respiratory problems but was revived by the hospital staff at Keswick Intensive Care Unit. Or so we were told!

At the age of twelve, I had to don a red woollen bathing suit and swim beneath the surface of Coniston Water in search of pearls. One secret is that back in 1973 our construction team added quite an extensive shingle beach to Peel Island for me to set off from. I'm not sure if the National Trust would allow this today. The lighthouse tree I had to look around when we first spotted the Amazon pirates was a long log set up on a promontory overlooking *The Lady Derwentwater* which had been given the role of Captain Flint's houseboat. I delivered my lines with great speed. The log had been planted in a red ants' nest and they were not happy about it.

Disaster loomed when *Swallow*, our small sailing dingy, nearly collided with *M. V. Tern*, the Victorian steamer that still takes passengers up and down Windermere. We were meant to just miss hitting her in the screenplay. The reality was that we lost our wind and she nearly took us to the bottom of the lake.

We were also lucky. The opening scenes of our film were set on a steam train approaching Westmorland. The Lakeside and Haverthwaite Railway, with its authentic steam locomotives, had only just been restored. It had been running for two weeks. George Pattinson, who established the steamboat museum on Windermere, appeared in the Rio scene at the helm of his beautiful steam launch, *Elizabeth*.

A word of warning: the lanes of the Lake District are narrow, twisty and bordered with dry stonewalls of unforgiving nature. Long vehicles normally associated with film crews are not just at risk; they will get stuck. Instead of hiring trailers to shelter our wardrobe and make-up departments from the elements, we used two red double-decker buses. Watching them navigate Mrs Batty's curving farm drive was comic. It raised the morale of the whole crew.

Distances in Cumbria can be deceptive. Our opening scene was set at

Foreword

Friar's Crag up near Keswick. Attempting to drive there from Coniston in time to catch the setting sun caught us out twice and we ended up picking up the shot on a sunny morning in Surrey, which was rather a shame as otherwise we could claim that *Swallows and Amazons* was shot exclusively on location in Cumbria. Rainy weather, busy roads and the sound of motor-boats can be a challenge but the grandeur of lakes and mountains transcends mundane problems. You will need an energetic location manager and up to three options on the call sheet but if you want to make a film for the big screen, why would you *not* want the ever-changing backcloth provided by the regal landscapes of Cumbria? And rain or shine, you will have fun.

Sophie Neville, August 2015.

AN A TO Z: CUMBRIA AND THE LAKE DISTRICT ON FILM

Introduction

IT'S easy to understand why so many artists and filmmakers continually regard Cumbria and the Lake District with great affection. The distinctive landscape is a strikingly beautiful world of mountains, lakes and dales and is normally so breathtaking it is often the main scene-stealer itself. Chris Noonan (director of the hugely successful biopic Miss Potter), perhaps summed it up best, when he described the region as one of the most 'spectacular on earth'.

Yet, for all the hundreds of literary guides or online sources to this ever popular landscape, so far, a comprehensive guide bringing together its varied film and social history with details of all the locations has not been produced. A traveller highlighted the issue on an internet travel forum recently, 'I was wondering if anyone knows of any movies that were filmed in Cumbria's Lake District?' The first reply suggested Bruce Robinson's unforgettable *Withnail and I*, released back in 1987, whose less than delightful weekend in the country has since achieved cult status. However, the same message mistakenly advised that the legendary tea room scenes were also filmed in Cumbria (you know the bit where Withnail delivers the immortal lines, 'We want the finest wines available to humanity, we want them here, and we want them now!') For those in the know, the scene was actually constructed from an empty store now home to Cox & Robinson's Chemist at 1 Market Square, in Stony Stratford, a village near Milton Keynes!

Other replies mention the enchanting tale of how such celebrated children's characters as Peter Rabbit and Jemima Puddleduck were brought to life on the silver screen in Noonan's *Miss Potter*. A film about the ideal summer holiday, Arthur Ransome's *Swallows and Amazons* is also widely acknowledged. The earliest of his series of much loved books, it was first adapted for cinema in 1974. A new adaptation by Harbour Pictures and BBC Films was shot in 2015, and the story remains as much a part of any child's library as Beatrix Potter's famous little books.

The terrifying rage virus unleashed in Danny Boyle's British horror film *28 Days Later* from 2002 is hailed as the most popular search result, whilst parts of Karel Reisz's intertwined love stories from John Fowler's literary classic *The French Lieutenant's Woman* are also highlighted. However, it soon becomes evident that this handful of recommendations provides only a tiny snapshot of feature films that have used Cumbria and the Lake District as a location.

The story of Cumbria and film really begins at the onset of the Second World War in a coal mine near Workington, with the filming of *The Stars Look Down* (1939). Great Langdale makes an appearance in Noel Coward's epitome of a bygone era, *Brief Encounter* (1945), whilst one of its co-stars Trevor Howard goes on the run with Jean Simmons through the heart of the Lakes in the fast-paced thriller, *The Clouded Yellow* (1950). More recently, Snow White and an alien mother inhabit abandoned slate quarries in the lavish adventure *Snow White and the Huntsman* (2012) or the low budget *Alien Blood* (1999), Bollywood takes over the Ullswater Steamer service; a fabulous stately home is overrun by drugged-up tormentors in *Killer's Moon* (1978); and the home of the world's first pencil features in the black comedy *Sightseers* (2012). Even the terraced streets of Denton Holme in Carlisle are used to depict the 1950s childhood of Carlisle-born director Mike Figgis in *The Loss of Sexual Innocence* (1997).

Not long ago, in a valley (not so) far, far away, one of the area's biggest film coups arrived when the all-conquering Star Wars franchise (reinvigorated by Disney) showcased the stunning backdrops of Derwentwater and Thirlmere. With close to 70 million views worldwide, the second official online teaser trailer for *Star Wars: Chapter VII – The Force Awakens* (2015) easily became YouTube's most viewed video of the summer. Both trailers featured clips of X-wing fighters descending across the surface of the two lakes doubling as a water planet. It really is a mouth-watering prospect envisaging the impact a cultural phenomenon such as Star Wars will bring to the Lake District.

The region also boasts a few links with the world's greatest detective. Firstly, when Michael Caine played a rather sozzled version of Holmes by the shores of Windermere in *Without a Clue* (1988). Or more recently, when Andrew Scott (best known for playing his arch rival Jim Moriarty in the BBC series *Sherlock*) arrived to cast a secretive shadow over the new version of *Swallows and Amazons*. Finally, there has to be a mention for the huge contribution made by Britain's most controversial and visionary director. Ken Russell arguably did more than most to put the Lake District firmly on the film map.

The aim of this A-Z guide is to show exactly how many filmmakers have been repeatedly drawn to Cumbria's definitive 'sense of place.' Despite the often unpredictable and wet weather conditions, directors and

INTRODUCTION

producers have repeatedly left the confines of their studios to show off some of the most dramatic backdrops in Britain. In the process they have helped to both inspire and fuel the imagination of audiences worldwide. According to the British Film Institute (BFI), one in ten foreign visitors come to Britain as a result of seeing the country depicted on the silver screen.

In a recent 'Screen Tourism' report for Creative England in association with Visit England, the results found that filming in the UK reached record levels in 2014, with international screen tourists contributing between £100-£140 million to the economy. A phenomenon known as 'set-jetting' has been consistently driving international tourists to some of the most popular locations, injecting up to £1.6 million a year in extra revenues. Films made in Cumbria have repeatedly boosted tourism, drawing the crowds because of their highly distinctive qualities. Majestic panoramas of lakes and mountains, isolated cottages, old packhorse bridges or the romantic melancholy of former slate quarries flicker across the region's cinematic life. A large variety of these locations have often become characters in their own right, combining tales of historical fiction, romance and adventure.

In the following pages you will find the stories behind the films alongside stills, photographs and maps of locations used. These provide insights into the history of cinematic places, which make up one of the loveliest corners of England. It is not meant to be a definitive film and location guide, more of a beginning. Nevertheless, through extensive research, speaking to directors, producers, location managers and local people, the cultural significance of Cumbria's rich cinematic history is brought to life here for the first time.

Cumbria and the Lake District
The stunning landscape of Cumbria is predominantly a rural one. At its heart is the Lake District (often simplified to The Lakes or Lakeland) one of Britain's most famous and popular holiday destinations. It also includes the Eden Valley (part of the North Pennines Area of Outstanding Natural Beauty), the Furness Peninsula, and 180 miles of coastline along the west coast, part of Hadrian's Wall, and a little slice of the Yorkshire Dales.

Established in 1951 and covering an area of 2,292 square kilometres, today the Lake District is England's largest National Park. It has many distinct advantages over potential rivals, being equally blessed with the highest mountain (Scafell Pike) and largest lake (Windermere) in England. Not to mention the variety of its landscape topography, where lush green beauty meets the rugged grandeur of an impressive army of mountains, reflecting back so dramatically on numerous lakes making the water appear like a large mirror.

Cumbria was formed back in the early 1970s when the old counties of Cumberland, Westmorland and parts of North Yorkshire and Lancashire combined to become England's second largest county. Lying close to the border with Scotland, the considerable city of Carlisle is the county town, with Barrow-in-Furness the second largest settlement area down towards the south western edge.

The history of Cumbria is a turbulent one, featuring numerous tales of battles and border raids between the 'auld' enemies of England and Scotland, along with some Roman and Viking invasions and settlements thrown in for good measure. At various times both kingdoms might have literally swallowed the other whole. In fact practically all of modern day Cumbria was under Scottish rule up until the Norman Conquest of England in 1066. Some historians have even declared that the Anglo-Scottish Border was one of the most notable creations of medieval Britain. Although a constant sea of political troubles on both sides of the border often led to violent skirmishes for the long suffering inhabitants of Cumberland and Westmorland.

Thankfully nowadays, the only hordes who come to visit are tourists. Drawn by the promise of the landscape as much as the area's cultural heritage, people crowd to see the houses and museums of William Wordsworth, John Ruskin and Beatrix Potter – a few of the most eminent literary figures associated with the area.

A

Across the Lake Tony Maylam, 1988
'With Donald, it's all or nothing!'

TV movie
Producer: Innes Lloyd
Photography: Andrew Dunn
Music: Maureen Darbishire, Richard G. Mitchell, Bryan Wade
Cast: Anthony Hopkins, Phyllis Calvert, Dexter Fletcher

Colour: 90 minutes
Screenplay: Roger Milner

A critically acclaimed feature-length film that details the final two months of the great British swashbuckling 'speed king' record breaker, Donald Campbell, played with ease by a suitably captivating Anthony Hopkins (*The Silence of the Lambs, Nixon*). The film recalls the lead up to events on 4 January 1967, (in near perfect conditions at Coniston Water in the southern part of the Lake District National Park), when Campbell set out to break the 300mph barrier

Bluebird's K7 replicated sponsons and conserved and straightened spars, © Anthony Stuchbury, courtesy of The Ruskin Museum, Coniston.

in the jet hydroplane *Bluebird K7,* hoping to further cement his World Water Speed Record. However, tragedy struck on the second run back across the lake, when *Bluebird* flipped up and incomprehensibly performed a full somersault before hitting the water in dramatic fashion. The impact killed the 46-year-old instantly and his story immediately became the stuff of legend. Since then, the manner of Campbell's untimely death, and colourful life, has found a lasting place in the national consciousness.

The film begins with a blue E-type Jaguar speeding its way along the serpentine B5285 towards the small village of Coniston in the Furness region of what would then have been Lancashire, (before it became part of Cumbria in 1974). Campbell (Hopkins) stops briefly, to stare pensively along the full length of Coniston Water, poignantly surveying the battleground of what will become his last hurrah. He drives over Yewdale Bridge, before pulling up at the Edwardian Sun Hotel, nestled snugly underneath the 2,634ft mass of Coniston Old Man. Most of the action unfolds in the hotel which has been providing hospitality to travellers for over 400 years.

The Sun Hotel was first known as the Rising Sun and then The Huntsman. It was also where one of Britain's best-known climbing clubs, the Fell and Rock Climbing Club held their inaugural meeting on 11 November 1906. The hotel's location on the old Walna Scar Road, which was a packhorse trail and trade route out towards the coastal ports, guaranteed it a healthy flow of regulars. From the 1860s, the Coniston railway encouraged increasing numbers of tourists, and the hotel had to extend to accommodate the demand. Since then, a Boat Room has been added above the bar, where a collection of unique, original photographs of Donald Campbell and Bluebird are on permanent display.

Campbell's playboy lifestyle is highlighted in the film when he begins an ill-fated affair with a London reporter Sarah Williamson (played by Julia Watson, probably best-known for playing Baz in the long running BBC drama series *Casualty).* The lifestyle is also on show when he obliges the flirtatious advances of petrol-pump assistant Judy (Juliette Grassby) who goes on to boast about 'having had the fastest man on the planet'. These illicit liaisons occur during an enforced separation from his wife Tonia Bern (Angela Richards) over the Christmas period.

As the drama of his last few days unfolds, Campbell becomes agitated by Sarah's rather unflattering 'Speed King in Turmoil' article. He has premonitions, and is constantly obsessed with superstition, seen in the ritual handing over of a teddy bear mascot known as Mr Woppit whenever he enters Bluebird's cockpit. On the fatal day itself, he lingers beside the lake once again to survey the clear and calm conditions of the mirror-like water.

English director Tony Maylam included lots of actual footage when reconstructing the last moments of Campbell's life. His previous 1987 film *Hero* (the official film of the 1986 World Cup held in Mexico) had featured

Diego Maradona's 'Hand of God' goal against England, another infamous moment in sporting history.

You can still see the sole remaining memento of the film at the excellent Ruskin Museum in Coniston. Placed amongst the artifacts in its specially designed 'Bluebird Wing' is a 'prop' sign with a map of Coniston Water along with the timing points for measuring kilometres.

The main part of the same display area is the real *Bluebird K7*'s replicated sponsons and conserved and straightened spars. A specially assembled 'Bluebird Project Team' continues to conserve and rebuild her hull. Eventually, they hope to run the real thing in low-speed engineering proving trials on Coniston Water, before installing a fully conserved and operational K7 on display at the Museum. There is also a film prop fibreglass replica cast in the Campbell display at the Lakeland Motor Museum at Haverthwaite. Various photos of Anthony Hopkins, as Campbell and himself, adorn the walls of the Black Bull pub and at the nearby Sun Hotel, both used as locations.

Coniston Sun Hotel, LA21 8HQ, OS ref: SD 30077 97323
The Ruskin Museum, LA21 8DU, OS ref: SD 30219 97663

Alien Blood Jon Sorensen, 1999
'The Truth is Out There…Way Out There!'

Certificate: 18 Colour: 80 minutes
Producers: Michael Herz (executive), Jon Sorensen
Screenplay: Jon Sorensen Photography: Peter M. Rowe
Music: Gary Lloyd
Cast: Francesca Manning, Rebecca Stirling, Glyn Whiteside.

With dialogue such as 'Do you like horses lad?' delivered by a sleazy farmer, there's really only one way British director Jon Sorenson's low-budget sci-fi encounter can go. Set on the eve of the new Millennium, the plot involves a pregnant alien's quest to board a mother-ship, while protecting her child and unborn baby. In the process they find themselves pursued by a moronic gang clad in black leather jackets, sporting white balaclavas, toting rifles and wearing dark shades.

Along the way, Helene (Francesca Manning) the alien mother and her infant daughter Monique (Rebecca Stirling), (both conversant in English and French for some unexplained reason) break into Dracula's house, where the Count (known as James) has assembled a gathering of bloodletting vamps to party into the 21st century. Helene promptly kills Dracula with a pistol, whilst the remaining vampires strip down into saucy negligees for a final shoot 'em up sequence with the advancing Men in Black balaclava troupe.

Shot entirely in the Lake District, the film used locations such as the iconic Kirkstone Pass and the relatively secluded Hay Bridge Nature Reserve, in the middle of the Rusland valley. Tucked in-between Windermere and Coniston, the reserve now houses a privately owned study and education centre. The stunning Furness Fells form a beautiful backdrop to an area already overflowing with a rich and varied selection of wildlife. In the film, they also provide a pleasant distraction from the roaming lunatics.

At the start there is a complete contrast to all the pastoral delights with a sequence shot exclusively in the lunar landscape of Hodge Close slate quarry, a former open and underground complex close to Coniston. Mining probably began there in the late 1780s, and continued with a few periods of inactivity until 1964. Helene and Monique meet a second alien mother with a child in tow in one of the quarry's dark caves. They end up bonding together beside

Skullduggery at Hodge Close © Unsworth Photographic.

a campfire, before exchanging numbers on massive, old-fashioned-looking mobile phones.

Today, the open pit is still flooded, just as it is in the scene when a hapless Helene stares vacantly into the void of the murky blue-green water. Back in 1915, the open quarry descended over 300ft deep, with just as much depth to the workings below. Ultimately, it proved a dangerous environment to work-in, particularly with all the potential rock falls. This led to the Buttermere Green Slate Company installing a so-called 'blondin' crane across the width of the pit in the 1920s to hoist slate from loaded tubs on the bottom of the quarry floor towards the top.

In recent times Hodge Close has gained a new notoriety, not only as a supernatural film location, but also as the place for a large number of climbing routes, where climbers continue to make good use of the precipitous rock faces. It has been popular with divers too, who often plumb the icy depths of the old flooded pit with its several deep chambers. Tragically, a number of climbing and diving fatalities have occurred on the site in recent years.

Ominously, in 2011, a national newspaper hailed Hodge Close as 'Britain's scariest cave'. A photograph capturing an eerie reflection contained echoes of Hans Holbein's famous painting *The Ambassadors* from 1533, that complimented the headline; both images revealing a skull, when flipped over or viewed from a slightly different angle.

Hay Bridge Nature Reserve, LA12 8JG, OS ref: SD 33680 87606
Hodge Close Quarry, LA21 8DJ, OS ref: NY 31743 01869

Axed Ryan Lee Driscoll, 2012

'His job kept him sane! Now he's just lost it...'

Certificate: 15 Colour: 84 minutes
Producer: Ryan Lee Driscoll Screenplay: Ryan Lee Driscoll
Photography: Edward Wright Music: Aleksander Dimitrijevic
Cast: Jonathan Hansler, Andrea Gordon, Nicola Posener, Christopher Rithin.

'Daddy knows best!' throughout independent filmmaker Ryan Driscoll's low-budget British slasher flick. The whole shoot on this darkened trip into the landscape lasted just over two weeks with a cast of six actors, a skeleton crew and hardly any time for rehearsals. The film was eventually released as part of a 'line-up to die for' under the renowned US film fan magazine *Fangoria Presents* Video-on-Demand (VOD) and DVD service. It was also the second title to be made available for all American Comcast subscribers, along with a host of other new and classic horror movies. *Fangoria* also produced a mini-issue

The isolated cottage © Shining Light Productions.

magazine based on the film, featuring interviews alongside comic book artwork provided by artist Mike Miller.

The film follows down-in-the-mouth Kurt Wendell (Jonathan Hansler) a project manager fired from his job in the big city who tries to hide the terrible news from his family. But as a result, he begins punishing those closest to him, making home life miserable for all. In the end, a gruesome fate awaits everyone, when he attempts to take his attractive wife (Andrea Gordon, from BBC's *Doctors*) and two teenage kids (Nicola Posener and Christopher Rithin) for a surprise day-off from work and school, into the countryside.

Kurt begins some family cut backs © Shining Light Productions.

They don't have to wait too long before the bloodletting starts in earnest. After they breakdown near a deserted cottage in the middle of nowhere, they begin to realise how much Daddy has really lost it.

The isolated cottage used for filming can be found at Hazel Head Farm, Ulpha, near Broughton-in-Furness. Inside it's a typical example of old Lakeland farmhouses: cold, damp and lacking in natural light. Perfectly matching Kurt's darkening mood.

Lying on the southern edge of the Lake District National Park, the area is surrounded by exquisite scenery, including the Furness fells and nearby Sandscale, North Walney and Hodbarrow nature reserves. Often hailed as one of the most attractive spots in the Lake District, the picturesque Duddon Valley is situated to the west of the quiet village of Ulpha. Wordsworth wrote extensively about the dale's river in his Duddon sonnets, following it on a fifteen mile journey from its highest point near the top of the Wrynose Pass down towards the Irish Sea. It encompasses a large part of the south-western fells: the eastern slopes of Ulpha Fell, the southern slopes around the head of Langdale and western slopes of Dunnerdale and Seathwaite Fells. Wordsworth's devotion to an area he knew with great affection from his upbringing in Hawkshead, led to him producing over 30 sonnets in praise of it. More recently, Norman Nicholson, Millom's favourite son, recounted a lifetime's knowledge of the valley in a number of poems not least his own 'To the River Duddon', which firmly embraced the tradition of Wordsworth.

Axed has a dark and disturbing storyline that sits somewhere in-between Joel Schumacher's *Falling Down* and Stanley Kubrick's *The Shining*. Kurt's *Jekyll and Hyde* mood-swings echo similar psychotic frustrations portrayed by D-Fens along with the increasing threats of violence Jack Torrance vents towards his own family.

Arguably the film's strongest point is the way it refuses to duck the major taboo of a father running amok and bumping off his own family. There is even a strong hint of incest added in for good measure, when Megan puts on Kurt's lunchtime present, a revealing red bikini. Before taunting him, "Isn't this what you really wanted Daddy?" In an interview in the *Fangoria Presents* publication, Jonathan Hansler admits to being a big fan of *The Shining*, citing Jack Nicholson's portrayal of Mr. Torrance as a major influence on the depiction of Kurt. Back in 1980, issue seven included a cover story on Kubrick's adaptation of Stephen King's best-selling novel, an event which marked the first time an American magazine had completely dedicated itself to the horror genre. It also became the first issue of *Fangoria* to make a profit.

Ulpha, Broughton-in-Furness, LA20 6DX, OS ref: SD 19823 9346

B

B. Monkey Michael Radford, 1998
'Trouble never looked so good...'

Certificate: 18   Colour: 92 minutes
Producers: Laurie Borg (co), Nik Powell (executive), Colin Vaines, Bob Weinstein (co-executive), Harvey Weinstein (co-executive), Stephen Woolley
Screenplay: Chloe King, Michael Radford, Michael Thomas
Photography: Ashley Rowe   Music: Luis Bacalov, Jennie Muskett
Cast: Asia Argento, Rupert Everett, Jared Harris, Jonathan Rhys Meyers

Michael Radford's 1994 film, *Il Postino: The Postman* won an Oscar for best original dramatic score, and was nominated in four other categories (including best director). However, there would be no such recognition for his next big screen production some four years later, the intriguingly titled *B. Monkey*. Based on a novel by Andrew Davies (a stalwart of TV costume drama, and the *Bridget Jones'* films), Radford stepped in to replace the original director. Michael Caton-Jones (*The Jackal, Memphis Belle, Rob Roy*) was first slated to direct *B. Monkey* but left the project citing 'artistic differences'. The idea of casting Sophie Okonedo in the lead role (an actress he'd previously worked with in 1997's *The Jackal*) had proved Caton-Jones' undoing, and was ultimately rejected by Harvey Weinstein, head of Miramax Pictures and the financial muscle behind the film.

Once Radford had been appointed he moved quickly to assemble a strong cast featuring: Rupert Everett as Paul, a fatalistic pot smoking bi-sexual; Jared Harris (son of the late infamous Irish actor Richard) as Alan, a straight-laced introvert; Jonathan Rhys-Meyers as the young whippersnapper Bruno (Alan's sometime boyfriend); Eddie Marsan as a thug; and a gorgeous, raven haired 21-year-old Italian actress Asia Argento (daughter of horror maestro Dario) as Beatrice, aka B. Monkey, a talented thief.

Billed as a romantic crime thriller, the film was never fully released in the UK. An inane plot didn't help a flat and laboured story, in which the main characters couldn't be further apart. Alan is a boring schoolteacher who plays late night jazz on hospital radio, whereas Beatrice or Bea is a sexy bank-robbing criminal. They end up together after an improbable encounter. Alan follows Bea out of his local pub after she looks to escape sometime friends, Paul and Bruno (themselves, an extremely camp and hammy pair of criminals).

She wants to quit crime and is after a nice, steady and reliable guy to settle down with, whilst he is longing for a bit of excitement. Alan soon becomes aware of Bea's shady past and attempts to take her away from it all (even though it may bring the kind of excitement he has supposedly craved). The story then moves away from the dark, rain-soaked London streets to the open fells of the Cumbrian countryside. Alan takes a job at a primary school in

Inside and outside a derelict Mountain View, near Narthwaite.

Sedbergh, a small and ancient market town in Cumbria but also within the Yorkshire Dales National Park, and surrounded by stunning moorland hills. Leaving the city behind, the couple rent an isolated farm – Mountain View, near Narthwaite, Sedbergh.

Nowadays the farm buildings are deserted, except for a few buzzards loitering menacingly overhead, making nervy rabbits scurry around carefully under the rotting floorboards. A general state of decay has long since set-in, with part of the roof fallen-in and the building open to the elements. Yet, even now there are still a few traces left over from filming: the distinctive narrow hallway remains intact along with the striking blue colour that Bea paints the walls of the lounge. You may still find a pleasant walk along the only track leading up to the old farmhouse by detouring from nearby Kensgriff in the resplendent Howgill Fells.

In the film's climax, trouble finds the couple once again when Beatrice foolishly contacts Paul, who simply traces the call back to locate the pair. Soon enough, he arrives with Bruno and a couple of other heavies from London. After a shoot-out ensues in the hallway, Alan and Beatrice are the last one's standing. Finally, they can relax in their rural paradise, although Bea's last line 'Whoever thought I could find happiness in the middle of fucking nowhere?' hints at a somewhat bittersweet recognition at the turn of events. B. Monkey? Behave!

Cross Keys, near Narthwaite, LA10 5NE, OS ref: SD 69800 96900

Bollywood in the Lakes

Lamhe   Yash Chopra, 1991
Certificate: U   Colour: 187 minutes
Producers: Yash Chopra, T. Subbarami Reddy (associate)
Screenplay: Honey Irani, Rahi Masoom Reza (dialogue)
Photography: Manmohan Singh
Music: Hariprasad Chaurasia, Shiv Kumar Sharma   Cast: Anil Kapoor, Sridevi

Mr Bhatti on Chutti   Karan Razdan, 2012
Colour: 102 minutes   Producer: Ashwani Chopra
Screenplay: Karan Razdan   Photography: Aatish Parmar
Music: Channi Singh
Cast: Anupam Kher, Bhairavi Goswami, Shakti Kapoor, Emma Kearney

Mujhse Dosti Daroge   Kunal Kohli, 2002
Certificate: U   Colour: 149 minutes
Producer: Yash Chopra   Screenplay: Aditya Chopra, Kunal Kohli
Photography: Ravi K. Chandran, Gopal Shah
Music: Babloo Chakravorty, Rahul Sharma
Cast: Rani Mukerji, Hrithik Roshan, Kareena Kapoor

Nammanna   Nimmala Shankar, 2005

Colour: 137 minutes
Screenplay: Goturi, Gurukiran, Kaviraj
Cast: Sudeep, Anjala Zaveri, Fllora Saini

Producer: Balamuttaiah
Music: Gurukiran

2013 marked the 100th anniversary of the first ever Bollywood film, D. Phalke's *Raja Harishchandra,* a silent black and white made during the heyday of the British Raj. In modern cinematic terms, few can doubt how far Indian cinema has come since that landmark moment. During the 1970s, it even overtook Hollywood (its main counterpart) as the largest film industry in the world, with Bollywood (its massive Mumbai-based operation) the most prolific in the country. Ironically, the name Bollywood was actually derived from an amalgamation of the former Mumbai (Bombay) and Hollywood. Now a huge powerhouse of cinema, it produces an estimated 1,000 films per year, and has an annual audience of 3 billion people. Easily overtaking Hollywood's 2.4 billion back in 2004; therefore, it goes without saying, Bollywood is a very lucrative market.

Lavish song and dance numbers are one of the recurring motifs in practically all of the films. There are literally thousands featuring musical scenes set against the romantic backdrop of lakes and mountains. Yet, sadly only a handful of films to date, have chosen to exploit the rich natural beauty that Cumbria and the Lake District can offer.

One of the great Bollywood director's Yash Chopra did try his best to put the Lake District on the map by filming scenes from two of his trademark romances at Ullswater. The classic *Lamhe* (Moments) from 1991 includes a lengthy song and dance routine performed by Sridevi and Anil Kapoor on the rolling slopes beside the region's second largest lake. Sridevi, (a former child-actress turned Bollywood superstar), went on to marry her frequent co-star's older brother, Boney Kapoor in 1996. Anil became best known to British audiences for playing 'Prem' in Danny Boyle's 2008 multi-Oscar winning film *Slumdog Millionaire*.

Although Chopra lamented that *Lamhe* had not been a great success in his native India, it still remained his own personal favourite film. He returned to the Lake District over a decade later as producer on the 2002 *Mujhse Dosti Karoge!* (Will You Be My Friend!), which took nearly one million pounds in the UK alone. Once more Ullswater predominated; during a song and dance routine performed onboard a steamer negotiating its way across the choppy waters. In a tribute to his earlier film *Lamhe*, the film's trio of main characters; Raj, Pooja and Tina, re-visit similar looking grassy banks beside the lake. Only this time they have a few scattered sheep for company and a tasty looking picnic spread out behind them. The film's enduring appeal was highlighted in 2015, when it was listed in *Time Out*'s countdown of the 100 Best Bollywood movies ever made.

Nammanna, Bollywood in the Lakes,
© *Gordon Shoosmith/Alamy Stock Photo.*

In November 2005, Hyderabad based director Nimmala Shankar's action drama *Nammanna* (Our Brother) was released. It remains his only film to date in the Kannada language, which is predominantly spoken in the southern Indian state, Karnataka. A mostly lacklustre and predictable plot features the character Muttanna, an innocent tribal man played by Sudeep, (a hugely respected figure in Kannada movies as an actor, director, producer and singer), who turns to violence in search of justice for his brother's killing. However, one of the film's main highlights is a memorable song and dance routine shot in beautiful bright sunshine at Bowness Bay, undoubtedly one of the Lake District's tourist 'honeypots'. With panoramic views of the fells and easy access to the shores of Lake Windermere, holidaymakers flock en masse to the bustling town every year. Awaiting them is an assortment of shops, restaurants and traditional inns, along with the opportunity to escape it all by hiring a motor or rowing boat or taking a lake cruise to Ambleside in the north or Fell Foot in the south.

Shankar chose to shoot an eye-catching piece of Bollywood cinema at the same spot where tourists usually go to eat ice creams or feed the ducks and swans. Throughout the playful song 'Chellu Chellu', actress Anjala Jhaveri's striking yellow sari perfectly compliments the deep blue skies and stunning view of the central mountains as she frolics on a jetty with Sudeep. The resulting images delightfully encapsulate Bollywood in the Lakes.

Karan Razdan's 2010 comedy, *Mr Bhatti on Chutti* (Mr Bhatti on Holiday) remains the only Bollywood production to film almost exclusively in Cumbria to date; although they had to overcome a number of delays due to problems with censors over the explicit use of a couple of leading politician's names. Eventually the film came out in May 2012, after the filmmakers extracted the names of former US President George W. Bush, and Indian Prime Minister Manmohan Singh from the dialogue. The film's story revolves around a group of Indian tourists who win a holiday to the Lake District. Soon after their arrival in Cumbria, they become mixed-up in the saga of a missing British woman. The opening song and dance routine really sets the farcical tone, with the comical refrain, 'Bhatti is gonna getcha!'

Veteran Bollywood actor Anupam Kher headed up the cast as Mr Bhatti, whilst sometime Emmerdale actress Emma Kearney landed her first ever role in Bollywood film as ditzy blonde, Alice. In 2004, Kher received the Padma Shri award from the Indian Government for his outstanding contribution to Indian cinema. A veteran of nearly 500 Hindi films, he also has a number of international films under his belt, including British director Gurinder Chadha's two big hits: *Bend it like Beckham* (2002) and *Bride and Prejudice* (2004) along with American director David O. Russell's 2012 Oscar nominated, *Silver Linings Playbook*.

The locations used in *Mr Bhatti on Chutti* include a number of trademark Cumbrian places alluding to wealth and tradition. Many other Bollywood productions are similarly renowned for putting opulent displays of cultural heritage in their films. There are four large hotels: Swallow Hilltop in Carlisle, Inn on the Lake at Ullswater, Storrs Hall at Windermere and The Langdale in Great Langdale. Once again, the Ullswater steamers are called into service, whilst scenes around Botchergate in Carlisle's city centre predominate towards the end: around the Lanes shopping centre, outside Woodrow Wilson's Wetherspoon's pub, Thongs n Things and two nightclubs – Club Cassa and Mood (now closed). Of course, the producers still found time to film at Knipe Hall, a grade II listed traditional farmhouse in the Lowther valley.

Brazil Terry Gilliam, 1985

'Somewhere in the 20th century'

Certificate: 15   Colour: 132 minutes
Producers: Patrick Cassavetti (co), Arnon Milchan
Screenplay: Terry Gilliam, Tom Stoppard, Charles McKeown
Photography: Roger Pratt   Music: Michael Kamen
Cast: Jonathan Pryce, Robert De Niro, Kim Greist

Terry Gilliam's classic retro-futuristic masterpiece *Brazil* ends with a fantasy dream sequence where Sam Lowry (Jonathan Pryce) and Jill Layton (Kim Greist) ride off into the idyllic landscape of the northern Lakes. With increas-

Sam's final delusion - the Newlands Valley from Newlands Hause.

ing desperation the pair try one last attempt to escape the clutches of an oppressive bureaucracy and the jackbooted thugs of the Ministry of Information. They attempt to do it in an S24 Scammell Commander Tank Transporter, except their cargo is a mobile home instead of a tank.

Eventually they stumble upon a suitably isolated cottage in the undulating landscape, where a contented plume of smoke billows out of a rather fake looking chimney. However, it turns out this escape to the country is nothing more than the hallucinations of an insane man. Fittingly, American born British director Gilliam chose to film Sam's final delusion in the scenic and pastoral Newlands valley, situated close to the popular market town of Keswick, in the north western Lake District.

The picturesque Newlands Pass also dissects this relatively quiet valley. A narrow three-mile strip of road stretches out from Braithwaite (a small hamlet situated north of Keswick) before eventually arriving at Buttermere. A popular Newlands horseshoe walk includes magnificent views from the summits of: Robinson, Dale Head, High Spy and Maiden Moor, whilst the distinctive humps of family favourite Cat Bells, await a little further on, near to Little Town, where the long walk usually begins.

Problems with the film's length caused quite a lot of controversy and became reminiscent of the difficulties encountered by fellow British director Ridley Scott who experienced similar run-ins with film executives on the Sci-Fi classic *Blade Runner,* originally released just a few years before in 1982. Although 20th Century Fox in Europe had put out *Brazil* in its original 142-

minute entirety, Universal Pictures handled distribution in the US. Unfortunately, their chairman Sid Sheinberg refused to release Gilliam's first cut. In essence, Sheinberg wanted a happy ending, Gilliam didn't, and as neither of them would give in, a year long stalemate began, which saw Universal shelve the project.

To provoke ridicule and embarrassment, Gilliam took out a whole page advert in *Variety* magazine asking Sheinberg famously, 'When are you going to release my film *Brazil*?' The Los Angeles Film Critics Association then turned up the heat on Universal by bestowing on the film its 'Best Picture' award, even though it had still not been released in the US. A couple of weeks later Sheinberg finally caved in and authorised the release of a 131-minute cut supervised by Gilliam. Twenty years on in 2005, *Time* magazine's film reviewers named it in an unranked list of the 100 best films of all time.

Newlands Valley, Newlands Hause, CA13 9XA, OS ref: NY 19274 17615

Brief Encounter David Lean, 1945
'A story of the most precious moments in a woman's life'

Certificate: PG Black & white: 86 minutes
Producers: Noël Coward, Anthony Havelock-Allan (uncredited), Ronald Neame (uncredited)
Screenplay: Noël Coward (from the play *Still Life*), Anthony Havelock-Allan, David Lean, Ronald Neame, (all uncredited)
Photography: Robert Krasker
Music: John Hollingsworth (associate musical director)
Cast: Celia Johnson, Trevor Howard, Stanley Holloway

This classic and enduring film has now become synonymous with a bygone era, harking back with a nostalgic twinkle of the eye to a Britain long since gone. Famously, the film version of Noel Coward's celebrated portrayal of the epitome of English reserve and romance, started with an innocuous tiny piece of grit. Nothing more than a small piece of stone kicked-up by an express train steaming through a rural station. A country beset by an age of austerity is perhaps the only thing we have left in common with it today. Yet, who could forget the station tea rooms, where everyone naturally drinks tea (or nips of brandy), a Boots Lending Library, (Boots used to run commercial libraries in some of their larger stores before the council ones took over), and of course those awfully prim and proper sounding accents.

A common misconception about the film is that it was actually set in the 1930s, and not at the end of the Second World War when it was made. Cow-

Celia Johnson and Trevor Howard, © Carnforth Station.

ard's 30-minute stage play *Still Life* had been re-written and re-named with Celia Johnson (Laura Jesson) and Trevor Howard (Doctor Alec Harvey) cast in the lead roles. Under legendary British director David Lean's (*Lawrence of Arabia*, *Doctor Zhivago*) direction, it became the love story of how a man and a woman (both married separately with two children) meet in the refreshment room at Milford Junction railway station. Using his professional skills, Alec introduces himself to Laura by removing that infamous bit of dirt from her eye. A guilt-ridden, seemingly impossible and unconsummated affair ensues, centred on restraint and excess.

Even the station itself elicits a similar contrast between mundane branch lines, and the potential adventure offered by journeys further afield. *Brief Encounter* was filmed towards the end of the Second World War between February and May 1945, with the Carnforth/Lake District elements shot first in a bitterly cold February. Milford Junction, (in real life Carnforth Station in Lancashire), had been chosen for a number of reasons; principally its location in the north of England, being far enough away from the south-east coast in case of air-raids. Speaking about filming at Carnforth, writer-director Lean recalled how they would always know if any German planes were coming, due to all the lights blazing away during scenes!

Lean also reputedly wanted a station where the actors were able to run up and down slopes from subways to platforms. After all, it just wouldn't have looked right if Celia Johnson had had to negotiate steps instead. Other requirements included a station serviced by both local trains and fast, non-stop express trains. A feature that becomes all too clear at the end of the film when Laura almost throws herself under an express train. Lean himself thoroughly enjoyed witnessing the recurring spectacle of the *Flying Scotsman* whizzing through the station at one fifteen in the morning, recalling the excitement of holding onto Celia Johnson's arm whilst the famous engine roared past within six feet of the pair. Milford Junction also required a buffet, which would mark the beginning and end of Laura and Alec's affair.

What time is love? © Carnforth Station.

Present day Carnforth Station (on the cusp of the Cumbria/Lancashire border) has now become a place of celebrated film pilgrimage and one of the most iconic places to visit for fans the world over. From the 1970s onwards this achievement would not have seemed possible, with most of the station buildings falling into a state of disrepair. However, 2013 marked the tenth anniversary of the complete station and refreshment room renovation, along with the opening of a Heritage Centre housing five exhibition areas. A full refurbishment of the iconic platform clock that features so prominently throughout the film was also instigated at the same time.

Now visitors are able to see key locations and sample the *Brief Encounter* exhibition and gift shop, where the film plays on a continuous loop every day. What's even better is that it's all free! However, donations are always welcome (and needed), seeing as a number of volunteers give up their spare time to keep the film alive on a daily basis.

The Cumbrian location in the film is seen a couple of times. As the affair progresses, Laura and Alec reserve their secret liaisons for Thursday afternoons; taking in a trip to the cinema (to watch the aptly named *Flames of Passion*) or by messing about on rowing boats. At one such meeting they over-indulge in a champagne lunch, and take a drive out into the country in a small two-seater borrowed by Alec. During the trip they stop to linger at a cold 'little bridge and a stream', which is actually Middle Fell Bridge over Langdale Beck in Great Langdale, near to the Old Dungeon Ghyll Inn.

The lovers peer down into the rippling waters, studying the rocks and watching for a sign of fish, trying to forget the perils of their situation with a warm, contemplative embrace. A lovely example of an ancient packhorse bridge, probably made out of local river-washed boulders, its single-arch design is typical of many others throughout Lakeland. Some of the early bridges like the one at Middle Fell Farm will have been built at the same time as the farms lying close to them. Apparently, Laura and Alec's bridge had been widened at the end of the nineteenth century, along with similar looking bridges at Stockley Bridge and Watendlath. Great Langdale has itself witnessed many changes over the years. In the early eighteenth century there were eleven small farms positioned around the valley head. Yet, just a century later there were only four; the foundations of several abandoned farms remain as traces of the effects of economic decline upon the people who used to farm there.

The 'stone bridge' sequence was the last one to be filmed in the north, after the production company had already called time at Carnforth, (the rest being shot at the old Denham film studios in Buckinghamshire). However, due to poor light levels as a result of the winter weather, shooting the scene had to be delayed by a couple of days. Eventually, Lean had to take a chance and film in whatever conditions arose, in order to keep up with scheduled filming on Regent's Park boating lake at the end of February.

Middle Fell Bridge, Great Langdale in winter.

Another feature throughout the film is the choice of music insisted on by Noel Coward, who implored Lean to use Rachmaninov's melancholic Piano Concerto No. 2 in C Minor Opus18, as a constant refrain. This proved a highly unusual idea back then, for almost all background music at the time was especially written for films. However, Coward's inspirational choice fitted perfectly with the main themes of the film with its bottled-up emotive passion and wistful, romantic fantasy; its whirlpool of anxiety, capable of transporting you to another world beyond the ordinary. Ultimately, the music helps Laura to retrieve her emotions bringing the self-reproach and frustration of her plight back.

Intriguingly, *Brief Encounter* only managed a modest box office return, compared with the other romantic melodramas released at the same time, but went on to be nominated for three Oscars (including in the Best Director and Best Actress categories). A film full of unanswered questions, there is no doubting the way it continues to endure for successive generations; it was voted No. 2 in a list of the Top 100 films of the twentieth century produced by the British Film Institute at the turn of the millennium. In April 2013, it topped a *Time Out* magazine poll of the 100 Most Romantic films ever made. Honouring its Cumbrian connection, the Roxy cinema in Ulverston celebrated its 75th anniversary in 2012 with a special celebratory screening. And thanks to the ongoing legacy of Carnforth's wonderful Heritage Centre, visitors can still seek out the very same place where Alec agonisingly squeezed Laura's shoulder goodbye.

Carnforth, LA5 9TR. OS ref: SD 49723 70678.
Middle Fell Bridge, Langdale, LA22 9JU. OS ref: SD 49723 70678.

C

Century on the Crags
William Cartner, 1986
'No man is a hypocrite in his pleasures'

DVD
Format: PAL
Manufacturer: Striding Edge

Colour: 53 minutes
Region code: Region 2

A seminal documentary film tracing the history of rock climbing, presented by the late Alan Hankinson (1926-2007). A fine climber himself, Hankinson (who somewhat appropriately lived on Skiddaw Street in Keswick) expertly outlines the story of the sport through the exploits of top climbers from each succeeding generation. With a distinguished career in TV, film, radio and journalism, it was as an author, that he produced the classic *Coleridge Walks the Fells* in 1984. A book that retraced the steps taken by Samuel Taylor Coleridge in 1802, where the Romantic poet made the first recorded ascent of Scafell, comparing the same places now with how they were just over 200 ago. Initially only available on video, *Century on the Crags* was released by Wasdale's Striding Edge Limited on DVD in 2005. It had been born out of an earlier book *The First Tigers: The Early History of Rock Climbing in the Lake District* first published back in 1972, where Hankinson profiled the pioneers of the 'golden age' at the dawn of the sport. Incidentally, the name 'Tiger' was applied by Peter Crew in his *Encyclopaedic Dictionary of Mountaineering* to mountaineers who were deemed to have climbed at a consistently high standard.

With a flowing mane of silvery-white hair, a number of vintage lumberjack shirts, old-school NHS styled specs and trademark deep-voice, 'the Hank' exudes a warm intelligence on-screen and is instantly likeable. He introduces the fascinating story at Wasdale Head, the centre of Lakeland climbing and so-called 'adventure playground of the pioneer rock climbers.' Filmed entirely in the Lake District, the DVD features contemporary climbers tackling the death defying breakthrough climbs along with numerous historic photographs and archive film footage.

Hankinson details how the first solo ascent of the remarkable detached pinnacle of Napes Needle on Great Gable in June 1886 by W. P. Haskett Smith (often referred to as the 'Father of English rock climbing') created a lot of interest, and was perhaps the true beginning of the sport. What looks particularly poignant in the film is the ascent of Napes Needle in 1913 by George and Ashley Abraham ('the Keswick brothers'). Filmed just before the outbreak of World War I, this is undoubtedly some of the earliest rock

Abraham Brothers photograph of first believed ascent of Kern Knotts Crack, 1897.

climbing footage ever produced. Hankinson typically draws our attention to how the intrepid duo are uncluttered by modern gear and afforded no protection whatsoever. These historic images could also be said to mark the true beginning of Cumbria on film.

The Abraham brothers also became superb photographers as shown in their iconic photograph of O. G. Jones's first ascent on Kern Knotts Crack (on the flanks of Great Gable) in 1897. This amazing shot, along with many other inspiring images, would help to promote the sport to a much wider audience.

Although now showing obvious signs of age, this landmark film is still a must-see for anyone remotely interested in how rock climbing evolved. It depicts relatively easy scrambles to routes still classified as 'very severe' out on the open cliffs and crags of the Lake District.

❧ ❧ ❧ ❧ ❧

Cheeky David Thewlis, 2003
'Some pieces of your life will never make sense'

Certificate: 15 Colour; 94 minutes
Producers: Luc Besson (co), Miara Martell (line), Trudie Styler, Anita Sumner (associate), Travis Swords
Screenplay: David Thewlis Photography: Oliver Stapleton
Music: Dario Marianelli
Cast: David Thewlis, Johnny Vegas, Trudie Styler

Filming for the well-known British actor David Thewlis's directorial debut coincided with the onset of winter in November in 2002. For many of the scenes, several shops and buildings in the bustling town of Ambleside in the central Lake District were transformed into a fictional town. Yet, to locals at least, the unnamed town was still instantly recognisable. The filmmakers had decided to use Ambleside purely for aesthetic reasons, citing the beauty of its buildings constructed mainly in local green slate. This fitted perfectly with the personal vision Thewlis had, which involved shooting in a town with a beautiful backdrop rather than depicting yet another gritty, northern industrial landscape on film. He also wanted to promote the area's natural beauty, as he believed it should be seen more on the cinematic screen. Filming lasted for two weeks, in wet conditions; except for one much needed interlude when the sun shone brightly.

A number of well-known landmarks were used, including the frontage to Fellinis independent cinema, Sir Giles Gilbert Scott's nineteenth century church of St. Mary's, and the CE primary school playground on Vicarage Road. Scenes (including the house fire) were also filmed on Millans Park,

Fellinis Cinema, Ambleside.

the same road where a blue plaque on number four now marks the former house of Merz-artist Kurt Schwitters. He was one of the major artists of European Modernism, who moved to Britain as a German refugee in 1940, and lived out the last couple of years of his life in Ambleside, before he died at Kendal hospital in 1948.

Thewlis originally wrote the screenplay in a hotel room over a three month period back in 1994-95. However, things didn't get moving until his former girlfriend, Anna Friel, told fellow actress Trudie Styler about the unused script during filming for *Me Without You* in 2001. Styler was impressed and agreed to co-produce the film with French director/producer Luc Besson (*The Fifth Element*), whilst taking the part of Nancy Grey. Within a year *Cheeky* was in production. Without intending to, Thewlis ended up playing the lead role of Harry Sankey, a young father and toyshop owner trying to come to terms with the death of his wife after she is killed in a house fire. He eventually sets out to honour her last wish by competing on 'Cheeky' a crude, but hugely popular game show where contestants score points by insulting each other.

Thewlis was born David Wheeler in March 1963 on the Fylde coast in Blackpool, Lancashire, where his father Alec, (like Harry in the film) owned a toyshop. He grew up writing poetry and playing guitar in local bands before turning to acting after attending the Guildhall School of Music and Drama in London. Choosing to use his mother's maiden name he soon broke-through for his multi-award winning role as a vagabond with verbal diarrhoea in Mike Leigh's 1993 film *Naked*. Since then he has gone on to perform in a variety of hugely successful films including: five of the *Harry Potter* films, *The Boy in the Striped Pyjamas* and *The Theory of Everything*. He also wrote and directed the BAFTA nominated 1995 short film *Hello, Hello, Hello*.

Despite a strong all-British supporting cast featuring the likes of: Lesley Sharp, Ian Hart, comedian Johnny Vegas, Mark Benton, Eddie Marsan and a young Sean Ward as Harry's difficult son Sam, *Cheeky* remained unreleased in the UK, until it came out on DVD in 2007.

Ambleside, LA22 9BU. OS ref: NY 37666 04464.

ৡ ৡ ৡ ৡ ৡ

Cloud Cuckoo Land
Matt Dickinson, 2004
'The higher your dreams the further you fall'

Certificate: 12A Colour; 92 minutes
Producer: Chris Bradley, Tony Allen (associate)
Photography: Andy Martin Screenplay: Matt Dickinson, Steve Varden
Music: Andrew Lagowski, Artic Melvin, Ed Poole, Andy White
Cast: Steve Varden, Derek Jacobi, Boo Pearce

A landmark production, which admirably decided *not* to cast an able bodied actor to play a major role in the film with a disability. By doing so, it went much further than previous films such as: *My Left Foot* (1989) and *The Theory of Flight* (1998) which had both featured characters with disabilities. Co-written by Matt Dickinson and Steve Varden, the film was inspired by real events and relates the story of an aircraft enthusiast with cerebral palsy whose dream is to fly. Suffering with the same form of severe disability, Varden (in his first feature) also performed his own stunts playing the lead role of Sandy Kenyon.

A former Paralympian, his own childhood dreams had involved hang-gliding solo. As an adult, he eventually set up a charity to help other disabled people take flight and experience the feeling he described as, 'the ultimate in physical and mental freedom.' Sadly, most of the major studios interested in buying the film wanted Varden dropped from the starring role and replaced with a non-disabled actor. Thankfully, Dickinson a writer and film-maker who had previously filmed on the summit of Mount Everest (and worked extensively for National Geographic, the Discovery Channel and the BBC) ignored all of them.

The project gained a significant boost when the well-respected classical British actor Sir Derek Jacobi (*Gosford Park, Gladiator*) agreed to play Sandy's grandfather Victor for free. Other cast members included a number of British film and television actors who offered their services in a similar

Victor (Derek Jacobi) attempts to reassure Sandy (Steve Varden) with Lucy (Boo Pearce) looking on, whilst the crew set up for another flight sequence © CloudCuckooLand.

fashion, including: Graham Cowley who incredibly took the role of Cameron (Victor's hard-nosed boss) after bumping into the film crew whilst on a family holiday in the Lake District! Boo Pearce (a young Shakespearian actress) played Sandy's girlfriend Lucy, who overcomes her own prejudices to disabled people and Rosalind Blessed, (daughter of the rambunctious booming voiced actor Brian) in the part of Linda, an assistant who works at Sandy's care home.

AN A TO Z: CUMBRIA AND THE LAKE DISTRICT ON FILM

In the film, Sandy and Victor spend their weekends searching for World War II aircraft wrecks. When Sandy learns that a potentially valuable mystery wreck is still missing in the Lake District, he decides to leave behind the safety of his care home to try and find it alone.

Mainly shot in Cumbria throughout June 2002, a number of different locations were used around the UK including: Cornwall, Derbyshire, Hertfordshire and Suffolk. Sandy is first seen arriving in the Lake District at a bus stop outside Booths supermarket in Keswick, before he visits the busy main high street where the distinctive Moot Hall dominates. He meets Lucy at a café owned by Vijay (Kriss Dosanjh), which was actually filmed at the beautifully converted seventeenth century farm buildings of the Upfront Gallery, near Hutton-in-the-Forest, Penrith. Owned by John Parkinson, the gallery's rural setting is home to a Puppet Theatre and the Upfront Cumbrian Artists Open, which exhibits work from all over Cumbria every January and February.

Vijay introduces Sandy to a strange group of travellers who rent him a cheap, run-down caravan to stay in, before playing a vital role in his quest to find the wreck. Producer Chris Bradley stated in his film diary notes that the cast and crew had to be flexible enough to shoot at 34 locations in 34 days. This resulted in a hectic schedule, with early scenes filmed at the Heaves Hotel, a former Georgian mansion on the outskirts of Kendal. Whilst Carlisle Airport featured heavily, including the Microlite Training Centre, Tecflite Ltd Hanger 163, Haughey Airports Ltd and Solway Aviation Museum. Scenes were also shot at Latrigg Hang Gliding launch site, Lonscale Farm, Threlkeld and at Latrigg Cottage, Blencathra Centre, Keswick and at the RAF Millom Museum, Haverigg (which sadly closed in 2010). The car breakers yard where Sandy ends up with a slightly battered blue jeep to cruise rather illegally around the Lake District in was Edenhall Auto Salvage, Bonnie Mount, Edenhall. The scene where he ends up getting himself all grubby whilst looking desperately for signs of the wreck at a 'bog swamp', was filmed at Solway Moss Peat Bog near Carlisle.

Most of the hang-gliding scenes were shot at various locations around Brigsteer, overlooking the resplendent Lyth valley, near to Scout Scar. This sprawling limestone escarpment and Site of Special Scientific Interest is hugely popular with walkers and located just south of Kendal. It is also here where they spread Victor's ashes after he succumbs to a doomed battle with cancer. In his honour, Lucy reads out the famous aviation poem 'High Flight' whilst Sandy looks on cutting a lonely figure atop the windswept heights. The sonnet had been written in 1941 by a nineteen year old Pilot Officer named John Gillespie Magee Jr. who died as a result of a mid-air collision flying a Spitfire over Lincolnshire in World War II.

The film ends on a happy note when Sandy finally realises his dreams taking majestically to the air over Derwentwater with the distinctive outline of Cat Bells in view throughout. Ultimately, he disappears with Lucy into a glorious red sunset seeking to find 'Cloud Cuckoo Land' in a final flight sequence that landed at 1st field, Chamber Tenement, Brigsteer. Fittingly, the film had a Lake District premiere on St. Valentine's Day in 2004 at the Keswick Film Festival. It subsequently went on to win a Best Director award for Matt Dickinson at the Napa/Sonoma film festival in San Francisco, USA.

Keswick, CA12 5AQ. OS ref: NY 26767 23260.
Carlisle Airport, CA6 4NW. OS ref: NY 48255 60614
Upfront Gallery, Penrith, CA11 9TG. OS ref: NY 45302 35969.
Lonscale Farm, Threlkeld, CA12 4RY. OS ref: NY 31986 25330.
Brigsteer, LA8 8AP. OS ref: SD 48131 89461.

The Clouded Yellow Ralph Thomas, 1950
'Goes careering through tight places with the velocity of a train'

Certificate: U
Producers: Betty E. Box, Vivian Cox
Photography: Geoffrey Unsworth
Black and White: 95 minutes
Screenplay: Janet Green
Music: Benjamin Frankel
Cast: Jean Simmons, Trevor Howard, Kenneth More

In 2010, this British thriller was restored to its former glory, as a new DVD release meant an outing for the opening scene, mischievously cut in an earlier version. Directed by Ralph Thomas (probably best known for the seven Doctor series of films, including *Doctor in the House* and *Doctor in Clover* in the 1950s and 1960s) it also starred the excellent, but infelicitous pairing of Trevor Howard (*Brief Encounter*, *The Third Man*) and Jean Simmons *(Black Narcissus, Spartacus)*. Howard was actually sixteen years Simmons' senior playing the role of David Somers, an ex-spy who takes a modest short-term position to catalogue butterflies at a mansion in the Hampshire countryside. Here he meets Sophie Malraux (Simmons), an intriguing young woman whose peculiar behaviour appears to be brought on by her mistrustful guardians Mr and Mrs Fenton.

Sophie is then accused of murdering a vindictive gamekeeper named Hick, prompting an infatuated Somers to go on the run with her in order to protect his somewhat fragile new-found beauty. Soon enough a full-scale chase develops for the fugitive pair who resort to desperate tactics trying to stay one step ahead of the law. Scotland Yard dispatch ex-secret agent Willy Shepley, played by Kenneth More (*Reach for the Sky*) to keep tabs on the couple, but after heading north by boat to the grimy, nooks and crannies of post-war Newcastle, Somers and the newspaper's so-called 'butterfly girl' end up fleeing to the wide-open spaces of the Lake District. Here, they foolishly stop for a quick cuppa at an outdoor cafe by the western shore of Ullswater, before a group of overly inquisitive cyclists arrive and recognise them instantly.

Forced to move-on, they board an old Cumberland single decker bus towards Patterdale on the A592 before getting off almost immediately to hide in a roadside ditch. Next, they stop for a breather on the rocks above Aira Force, just a five-minute walk from the road and one of Lakeland's most famous waterfalls. Powerful and spectacular at 230 feet, the cascade gathers in the surrounding hills before thumping and plumping its fury down beneath a stone bridge into a beautiful wooded ravine littered with spruce, fir, pine and cedar trees. Today, you may even spot a few red squirrels scampering through the woods if you're lucky.

Somers and Sophie don't stay hidden there for long though, as they switch valleys before being spotted by a police helicopter attempting to scramble up another foaming waterfall. They pause for breath at the delightfully named Sour Milk Gill, famously called 'a broad stream of white snow' by Dorothy Wordsworth.

This waterfall is found en-route to a popular walk up to Easedale Tarn, a mile or so up the valley from the centre of Grasmere. Famously referred to by the essayist and critic Thomas de Quincey as a 'Chapel within a Cathedral' the tarn's large hollow crater pours out of a narrow mouth to feed the gushing stream below. Eventually David fakes injury stumbling around on the slippery rocks and is captured by the police, before he easily escapes, and the couple flee the Lake District on a Lancastrian coach bound for Liverpool. Here, the final showdown at the docks takes place.

Sour Milk Gill, Easedale near Grasmere.

Throughout the pursuit, one of the most interesting characteristics is the way Thomas's skilful direction highlights the bomb damaged industrial landscapes of post-war Liverpool and Newcastle against the sprawling untouched Lakeland scenery.

Aira Force, Ullswater, CA11 OJS. OS ref: NY 41896 20541.
Sour Milk Gill, Easedale, LA22 9QL. OS ref: NY 30777 08764.

D

The Dambusters Michael Anderson, 1955

'The story of the 'bombs that had to bounce' and the air-devils who had to drop 'em!'

Certificate: U Black and White: 124 minutes
Screenplay: R. C. Sherriff (Based on Wing Comdr. Guy Gibson's *Enemy Coast Ahead*)
Photography: Erwin Hillier Music: Leighton Lucas
Cast: Richard Todd, Michael Redgrave, Ursula Jeans

If *Brief Encounter* is a model of British reserve and romance, then *The Dambusters* is the epitome of a British war film. A true story from the Second World War, it features a heady mix of pluck, eccentricity and stiff-upper-lip attitude. Not to mention a dog called by the contentious N-word! Details of the RAF's 617 Squadron's daring raids were brought back into the public spotlight again during May 2013, when numerous celebrations took place across Britain to commemorate the 70th anniversary of the mission codenamed 'Operation Chastise'. Barnes Wallace (played in the film by Sir Michael Redgrave) invented the bouncing bomb, which was used to arm the Lancaster bombers sent to attack Germany's trio of Ruhr dams; comprised of the: Möhne, Eder and Sorpe.

The production company, Associated British had bought the film rights in order to cast Dublin born actor, Richard Todd (a war hero in his own right, as one of the first soldiers to parachute into France on D-Day) in the role of Wing Commander Guy Gibson. Curiously, they also appointed Michael Anderson – a relative unknown at the time, to direct the film. Although he did have a good pedigree from working as assistant director to David Lean on Noel Coward's patriotic naval film, *In Which We Serve* (1942). Much later he went on to direct *Logan's Run* (1976) a post-apocalyptic sci-fi classic.

Filming *The Dambusters* proved a tricky affair that required three Lancaster bombers flying at extremely low level in close proximity to each other. This took place often over water whilst being filmed from a fourth aircraft. Pilots based at RAF Hemswell in Lincolnshire took turns at the controls during the making of the film. Flying over Derwentwater and Windermere provided them with both an exhilarating experience and welcome change from their usual high level solo Canberra flights.

Low level filming with a second unit crew over Windermere was undertaken at the end of August when the Lancaster's were subsequently detached to RAF Silloth in Cumbria. According to Jonathan Falconer's book, *Filming the Dambusters,* the most intensive day for aerial filming in the Lake District took place on 4 September 1954, when almost six hours of low level footage was accomplished. As England's largest lake it's no surprise that Windermere's expanse features so prominently throughout the film; during the practice flights before the raid, and the actual bombing runs over the dams. Filming also took place over the Kirkstone Pass and across the distinctive craggy top of Helm Crag, overlooking Grasmere Lake, for a scene in which three Lancaster's fly in low level formation just after the Operations Room receive news of the Möhne dam breaking.

The cast and crew astride a Lancaster bomber,
© *1955 STUDIO CANAL Films Ltd.*

Some places in the Lake District received more than they bargained for during filming, according to Derek Browne, a camera operator shooting low level footage on-board one of the Lancasters. He recalled how a prank to bomb the Langdale Chase Hotel on the eastern shore of Windermere didn't go down very well! The incident took place when one of Europe's crowned heads of state was staying at the former country house. Unfortunately they received an unexpected memento of their stay, after being hit directly by a toilet roll thrown out of the bomb doors! Thankfully, guests at the hotel are much safer nowadays, and are far more likely to receive gifts from hosts at wedding ceremonies than any low-level flying WWII bombers. Naturally, Browne didn't escape without a ticking-off from his boss Erwin Hillier (Director of Photography) after a firm complaint had been lodged with the production office.

All of the 70th anniversary commemorative events may yet serve as a timely nudge to New Zealand director Peter Jackson, (current owner of the filming rights) whose long touted remake of the 1955 original has still to get off the ground. At present, 'script issues' have been cited as the main reason behind countless on-going delays. However, it is unlikely the project will get to see the light of day soon, as Jackson, (director of the multi-award winning *Lord of the Rings* and *The Hobbit* trilogy), although a self-confessed aeroplane obsessive, has already begun work on the sequel to *The Adventures of Tintin*.

Windermere, LA23 1AH. OS ref: SD 41383 98645.
Derwentwater, CA12 5UR. OS ref: NY 26000 20000.
Grasmere, LA22 9PZ. OS ref: NY 33679 07551.

The Darkest Light

Simon Beaufoy, Bille Eltringham, 1999
'It takes the faith of a child, to see the light'

Certificate: 12   Colour: 92 minutes
Producer: Mark Blaney   Screenplay: Simon Beaufoy
Photography: Mary Farbrother   Music: Adrian Johnston
Cast: Stephen Dillane, Kerry Fox, Keri Arnold

In 1997, a 30-year-old named Simon Beaufoy from Keighley, West Yorkshire, looked to have the film world at his mercy. Having just seen his debut script turn into a multi-million pound global phenomenon. The script in question was for *The Full Monty*, a heart-warming story set in Sheffield about a group of unemployed men (mainly ex-steel workers), who form a male striptease act in order to raise money for Gaz (the main character played by Robert Carlyle) to pay child support for his ex-wife. It became Britain's biggest film-hit at the time, only more recently surpassed by James Bond and some of the Harry Potter adventures. Curiously, Beaufoy chose to follow it up with the low-budget film *The Darkest Light*, which also marked his debut as a co-director with long-term partner Bille Eltringham.

The film is the story of a young Catholic girl named Catherine (Keri Arnold), the spirited daughter of Tom (Stephen Dillane – *Welcome to Sarajevo, The Hours*) and Sue (Kerry Fox – *Shallow Grave, Bright Star*) a struggling farming family from the North Yorkshire Dales. Her younger brother, Matthew (Jason Walton), is seriously ill with leukaemia, so when ten year old Catherine and her new Hindu classmate, Uma (Kavita Sungha), witness a strange and mysterious phenomenon on the moors, Catherine is convinced that the intense light she sees is a sign that Matthew is going to get better. On the other hand, Uma thinks something terrible is going to happen, and whilst news of the 'vision' spreads, Catherine remains positive that she not only holds the key to her family's uncertainties, but those of the whole community. Despite an outbreak of the dreaded foot-and-mouth disease at the family farm, Catherine's conviction that Matthew will be cured only gets stronger. Intriguingly, four years after shooting *The Darkest Light*, Dillane and Fox teamed up as husband and wife again in Brian Gilbert's middle-of-the-road horror suspense film, *The Gathering,* another story where visions are prevalent.

A number of different places were used during filming with the main production office set up in Sedbergh, which proved to be a successful base to find locations within easy reach of the town. The grocery store and post office ran by Uma's mother Nisha (Nisha K. Nayar) was filmed at Barbon, a small village in South Lakeland situated in the Lune Valley between Kirkby Lonsdale and Sedbergh. A remote farm in the North Yorkshire Dales between Ingleton and Chapel-le-Dale in the River Doe Valley doubled as Catherine's family home. Location Manager Christine Llewellyn-Reeve said it had been hard work to find, due to its isolated position nestled below the dominating backdrop of Scales Moor. They did receive a huge stroke of luck during filming when the family occupying the original nineteenth century farmhouse moved into a new one on the same site, giving the crew 'carte blanche' to use an empty house.

The quiet idyll of the countryside is immediately disturbed at the start of the film when a low-flying jet speeds over the iconic Ribblehead Viaduct on the Settle-to-Carlisle line – a common occurrence above the skies in the Lake District. Catherine's fictitious school is Horton-in-Ribblesdale Primary School, near Settle, in North Yorkshire. Matthew's funeral was also filmed in the small upland village at St. Oswald's Church and graveyard. Catherine and Uma wander around aimlessly at the well-known limestone pavement at Malham Cove, in the Yorkshire Dales on the top and base of the distinctive cliff formation as well as on adjacent farmland. Memorably scenes from Harry Potter's two-part film: *Harry Potter and the Deathly Hollows* were filmed there and at the nearby dramatic ravine Gordale Scar too.

Playing truant from school, the pair discover an empty tank at Warcop Army Training Ground, in the North Pennines Area of Outstanding Natural

The lonely ash at Malham Cove, © *Chris McLoughlin Wildlife and Nature Photography/Alamy Stock Photograph.*

Beauty. Situated between Appleby-in-Westmorland and Brough, the land covers an area of approximately 24,000 acres and is one of the largest army training areas in the UK. Established in 1942 as a tank gunnery range, almost all of the armoured formations used in the D-Day landings trained there before heading off to mainland Europe. Sue tells her daughter that her bone marrow is a match for Matthew's at the Culgaith Level Crossing, near Temple Sowerby and Penrith, on the Settle-to-Carlisle line. At the end of the film, Catherine is comforted by her father after Matthew's death at the former St. John's church in Windermere, which had been de-commissioned after closing in 1995. The production team built Matthew's scanner treatment room in a section of the old church. Other hospital scenes were filmed at The Westmorland General Hospital, Kendal.

Warcop Army Training Ground, CA16 6PA. OS ref: NY 74854 15777.
Culgaith, Penrith, CA10 1QF. OS ref: NY 60940 29180.
(Former) St. John's Church, LA 23 2EQ. OS ref: SD 40955 97751.

Deep Lies
Phil Stagg, 2009

'Romance, Reunion, Retribution'

Certificate: 15
Producer: Robbie Moffat
Photography: Bob Ramsay
Colour: 88 minutes
Screenplay: Phil Stagg
Music: James Chadwick
Cast: Marnie Baxter, Howard Corlett, N. Andrew Elliot

A thriller set in the Lake District, where a girls-only reunion turns into a murderous piece of retribution. Screened at the Cannes film festival in 2009, but unreleased in the UK, the film was written and directed by Phil Stagg, who'd previously worked on another north-west based release, *Barefooting (2008)*. Mostly filmed on or around Ullswater, other exterior shots included the bottom of Cat Bells near Hawse End, Tarn Hows and Penrith Railway Station. The story revolves around four girls embarking on an ill-fated reunion at the majestic Lodore Falls Hotel in Borrowdale.

The quaint hotel is situated in an exclusive position spectacularly overlooking Derwentwater, settled amongst a veritable amphitheatre of mountains. Built in distinctive Lakeland slate, its commanding presence next to the dramatic Lodore Falls has graced the area for over 200 years. During their time together, the girls also decide to take a trip out to the ancient monument, Castlerigg stone circle, built around 3000BC, on the outskirts of Keswick.

Tanya (far right) shares a bottle at Castlerigg stone circle
© *Palm Tree Entertainment.*

Although the stunning views across to Skiddaw, Blencathra and Lonscale Fell are seemingly ignored in favour of a large bottle of Smirnoff! *Got to Run*, another film produced by the same production company (Palm Tree Entertainment), shot scenes at Castlerigg a year later in June 2009.

Penrith Railway Station, CA11 7JQ. OS ref: NY 51205 29889.
Lodore Falls Hotel, CA12 5UX. OS ref: NY 26434 18871.
Castlerigg stone circle, CA12 4TE. OS ref: NY 28277 22495.

Downhill

James Rouse, 2014

'A road movie on foot'

Certificate: 15   Colour: 98 minutes
Producer: James Rouse
Screenplay: Torben Betts, Benjamin Howell, James Rouse
Photography: Alexander Melman   Music: Park Music
Cast: Ned Dennehy, Richard Lumsden, Jeremy Swift, Karl Theobald

At the end of May 2014, *Downhill* followed Terry Abraham's homage to Scafell Pike and children's favourite *Postman Pat: The Movie* as the last of three films to premiere in the Lake District. In what proved to be an unforgettable month for Cumbrian cinema, Zeffirellis independent cinema in Ambleside hosted a grassy red carpet affair held in aid of the Langdale and Ambleside Mountain Rescue Team. The dress code was simple, evening dress with walking boots or wellies! Billed as a bittersweet comedy, the film's story is about four old school friends approaching the age of 50, who decide to get together for the first time in 30 years to conquer one of the world's great walks, the celebrated Coast-to-Coast.

Devised by the legendary late fell walker Alfred Wainwright in a guidebook first published in 1973, the Coast-to-Coast is a gruelling 192 miles in length and passes through three contrasting national parks: the Lake District, Yorkshire Dales and North York Moors. However, since Wainwright's day it has had to be much revised due to increased road traffic and legal restrictions on footpaths. In 2010, a completely updated second edition by Chris Jesty was published, who also previously revised Wainwright's seven *Pictorial Guides*. A west to east route begins on the Irish Sea at St. Bees in Cumbria and crosses the Pennines, Yorkshire Dales, Vale of York and North York Moors before finishing on the North Sea coast at Robin Hood's Bay. Tradition dictates all coast-to-coasters dip their toes in the Irish Sea, whilst gathering a few pebbles to deposit triumphantly at the other end in the North Sea.

The film was shot in a fly on the wall documentary style, and it doesn't take long before the four main characters: Gordon played by Richard Lumsden (*Sightseers*), Keith by Karl Theobald (*Alan Partridge: Alpha Papa*), Steve by Jeremy Swift (*Amazing Grace*), and Julian by Ned Dennehy (*Sherlock Holmes*) realise how different their personal and professional situations have become over the intervening years. The journey is portrayed from the perspective of Gordon's son, Luke, who decides to document events for a college project. Along the way they encounter: Jen played by Emma Pierson (BBC TV's *Hotel Babylon*) and Caroline by Katie Lyons *(*Channel 4's *The Green Wing)* a couple of attractive young girls also attempting the walk. Sadly, they only serve to remind them of their collective loss of mojo. As the pilgrimage across the landscape unfolds, strains of work and family float to the surface, whilst a series of mid-life crises are painfully revealed.

The film project started as the brainchild of producer Benji Howell who had been mainly working on television commercials with London based director, James Rouse. Embarking on their first feature, they started to collaborate on an outline story before recruiting acclaimed English playwright Torben Betts to write the screenplay. Filming took place throughout June 2012, in what turned out to be the wettest June on record! Unsurprisingly, the difficult conditions often played havoc with the schedule and ruined some of the film rushes. Inevitably, the crew had to return in September of the same year to shoot a few additional scenes. With Rouse and Howell sticking as close to the walk as possible, the list of Cumbrian and Lake District locations will be most familiar to anyone who has undertaken the challenge. Beginning with the Heritage coastline of the red sandstone cliffs at St. Bees Head, the second day sees the quartet move into the middle of the Lake District and onto the slippery, misty slate-ridden paths of the Honister slate mine.

Keith begins the confessionals by 'coming out' to his best friend Gordon after a drunken evening at the White Lion Inn at Patterdale beside Ullswater. Unfortunately, their insecurities begin to flow along with the drinks. At breakfast the following morning Gordon holds a battered copy of Wainwright's guidebook above the first of many hearty looking fry-ups. There are passing references to the cult film *Withnail and I,* when a red phone box eats a few of Gordon's coins or in the character of Julian, whose Bohemian lifestyle and chain-smoking vitriol increasingly echoes Withnail's booze-fuelled outbursts.

Yet, if all the self-deprecating humour doesn't inspire, then the magnificent landscape scenery undoubtedly will. Other scenes were filmed at the supposedly haunted Edenhall Country Hotel, near Penrith, (where several ghosts are said to have appeared in mirrors above the bar!), the George Hotels in both Keswick and Penrith, Keswick Golf Club, the Queens Hotel, Keswick, the Scafell Hotel, Borrowdale (a renowned headquarters for fell walkers at the foot of Great Gable and Scafell), and at Shap Abbey Farm and Bowling Club. Of course, any coast-to-coast would not be complete without lashings of fish and chips at the finish. So the film ends appropriately enough with the

Downhill, from left to right, Gordon, Steve, Julian and Keith overlooking the Honister Pass, © Crisis Films.

foursome tucking-in, after somehow reaching the holy grail of the North Sea at Robin's Hood Bay.

St. Bees Head, CA28 9UY. OS ref: NX 93745 14927.
Honister Slate Mine, CA12 5XN. OS ref: NY 24471 13769.
White Lion Hotel, Patterdale, CA11 0NW. OS ref: NY 39677 15826.
Edenhall Country Hotel, Penrith, CA11 8SX. OS ref: NY 56579 32449.
Scafell Hotel, Borrowdale, CA12 5XB. OS ref: NY 25782 14829.
Robin Hood's Bay, YO22 4RE. OS ref: NZ 95160 05544.

F

The French Lieutenant's Woman

Karel Reisz, 1981

'She was lost from the moment she saw him'

Certificate: 12　　　　　　　　Colour: 124 minutes
Producers: Leon Clore, Geoffrey Helman, Tom Maschler
Screenplay: Harold Pinter
Photography: Freddie Francis　　　Music: Carl Davis
Cast: Meryl Streep, Jeremy Irons, Hilton McRae

Broad Leys is a large house overlooking the eastern shores of Lake Windermere. Czech director Karel Reisz deliberately chose the beautiful residence to shoot the last few scenes of his adaptation of the classic John Fowles novel. His specific intention had been to depict the home of an avant garde architect. Designed by C. F. A. Voysey, one of the leading figures of the Arts and Crafts movement, the exquisitely positioned house is now considered to be one of his finest. Situated on a narrow piece of flat land, he built it in 1898 as a weekend retreat for a wealthy Yorkshire coalmine owner, when the Lake District was becoming a popular holiday destination.

At the same time, all around Windermere several other prominent houses sprang up for the affluent upper-middle classes, who wished to own similar escapes from their industrial landscapes. Blackwell, designed by Baillie Scott and now owned by the Lakeland Arts Trust was built at the same time. Situated only a mile or so away from Broad Leys, it is another beautiful holiday home laced with outstanding representations of the Arts and Crafts style.

Voysey was hailed as a 'pioneer of modern design'. He preferred plain interiors, oak panelling, whitewashed walls, over-hanging eaves and broad chimneys; all trademark features on show at Broad Leys. In 1951 the house gained a new role as the headquarters of the Windermere Motor Boat Racing Club, whose long racing history boasts illustrious members such as Sir Malcolm and Donald Campbell. Nowadays the house is the only Voysey building in the world open to the public for either accommodation or private functions. The Windermere suite is the largest of three and offers superb panoramic views over the lake and gardens. It also affords visitors an opportunity to stay

The Windermere suite at Broad Leys today.

in the same room where the vision of a film director helped create a little piece of film history in the early 1980s.

The screenplay did contain a significant change from Fowles' book in which Charles Smithson eventually tracks Sarah Woodruff down in London rather than the Lake District, after she flees from their Exeter love-nest. One of the most talked about films of its time, *The French Lieutenant's Woman* contains a double story, which follows the nineteenth-century romance of Sarah and Charles, whilst a parallel thread shows the modern-day affair of Mike and Anna; two actors playing Charles and Sarah in a film production of the novel.

The film earned Hollywood superstar Meryl Streep a third Oscar nomination for the roles of Sarah/Anna, whilst the accomplished British actor Jeremy Irons co-starred as Mike and Charles.

There were further Oscar nominations for the reworked screenplay from celebrated playwright Harold Pinter, in best costume design, best film editing and in the best Art direction category for production designer, Assheton Gorton, an Old Sedberghian from the distinguished public school in Cumbria's Howgill Fells. Gorton was born in the school's Winder House in 1930 where his father was housemaster. Now he is regarded as one of the most important production designers in British Film history, with an impressive body of work ranging from: *Blow Up* (1966), *Get Carter* (1971), *Legend* (1985) and *Rob Roy* (1995).

Broad Leys, Windermere, LA23 3LH. OS ref: SD 39312 93263.
Blackwell, Bowness-on-Windermere, LA23 3JT. OS ref: SD 40163 94592.

G

The Gentle Sex

Leslie Howard and Maurice Elvey (uncredited), 1943
'Seven women whose lives are turned upside down'

Certificate: U   Black and White: 92 minutes
Producers: Derrick De Marney, Leslie Howard
Screenplay: Moie Charles   Photography: Robert Krasker
Music: John Greenwood
Cast: Joan Gates, Jean Gillie, Joan Greenwood

The film is a Second World War documentary-style piece of propaganda that deals with the transformative effect of the war on ordinary citizens. It attempts to do this by mainly portraying images of women working and performing similar roles to those of men in several different and challenging roles. The plot charts the experiences of seven women from a variety of backgrounds who join the ATS (Auxiliary Territorial Service) for a new and demanding way of life.

Their separation from civilian life is documented through a series of individual parting shots at a railway station, relayed by narrator and co-director Leslie Howard (who was tragically killed when his plane was shot down by the Luftwaffe on a secret mission to Portugal in WWII). Soon enough the women develop close-ties, safe in the knowledge they are all 'doing their bit' for dear ol' Blighty's war effort. However, as they begin to encounter each other at close quarters, tensions begin to rise and their togetherness is tested and inevitably becomes strained. Postings to various jobs throughout the country soon follow; although a few remain in the same place, whilst the rest are separated from the original group.

Cumbrian locations were filmed around the great border city of Carlisle as the army convoy passes along English Street (now the entrance to the Lanes shopping centre). Other scenes were shot at the battlements of the Castle, where a few of the ladies operate an anti-aircraft gun situated towards the rear, close to the sheep-mount.

Like the film *Millions like Us,* brought out in the same year, *The Gentle Sex* was ultimately concerned with change, posing the intriguing question of

An A to Z: Cumbria and the Lake District on Film

The Gentle Sex film poster.

whether the war's aftermath would alter women's position in the world for good.

Carlisle Castle, CA3 8UR. OS ref: NY 39645 56289.

I

If Only
Gil Junger, 2004

'He loved her like there was no tomorrow'

Certificate: PG-13 Colour: 92 minutes
Producers: Jennifer Love Hewitt, Gil Junger, Jill Gilbert, Jeffrey Silver
Screenplay: Christina Welsh Photography: Giles Nuttgens
Cast: Jennifer Love Hewitt, Paul Nicholls

Texas-born actress and musician Jennifer Love Hewitt produces, and plays American student violinist Samantha in this slushy romantic drama. Paul Nicholls (formerly 'Joe Wicks' in *Eastenders*) co-stars as Ian Wyndham, Hewitt's partner, whose ambitious career often makes him neglect her and take their relationship for granted. After forgetting her graduation ceremony they almost break-up in a restaurant, before Samantha gets in a taxi alone. She tragically dies when a car accidentally ploughs into the side of the cab.

Ian is initially disconsolate, but wakes up the next day to find Samantha miraculously back by his side. Somehow he has been presented with the chance to re-live the fateful day all over again, only this time in the hope of changing events that led to her death. Set almost exclusively in London, the story eventually moves up to the Lake District when Ian takes Samantha on a train journey for a swift trip up to his rural hometown. During this sequence we glimpse them somewhat half-heartedly attempting to make their way in trademark Cumbrian weather to a spot Ian used to visit as a child.

Getting soaked, they decamp to a hut near to a group of deserted slate quarry workings, halfway up a mountainside. Once inside, they are greeted by a seemingly abundant supply of firewood and candles left conveniently on the off chance, for whoever might drop in! These scenes were filmed near the Honister Slate Mine, the last working mine of its kind in England. Located in a rugged corner of the Lake District with large machinery still adorning Honister crag, it has now become an award winning visitor attraction. Mark Weir, a charismatic local businessman rescued the mine from bankruptcy in the late 1990s, before turning it into a thriving concern visited by some 60,000 people on an annual basis. Tragically, he was killed in March 2011 when piloting a helicopter close to the mine in poor weather conditions.

His legacy still lives on in the mine tours and according to Jules Brown (editor of Rough Guides) 'the Lake District's biggest thrill' is the Via Ferrata Classic and Xtreme – a challenging climb along a series of metal ladders and walkways leading up to the summit of Fleetwith Pike.

After drying out in their cosy slate hut, Ian and Samantha continue their intense day of sharing by heading across the magnificent double-arched bridge over the River Derwent at Grange in Borrowdale. Built in 1675, the bridge still serves as the entrance to the small hamlet of Grange, on the road out from Keswick alongside Derwentwater. Squeezed in-between Grange Fell and Castle Crag at a place once known as the Jaws of Borrowdale, it is quietly overlooked by the smooth slopes of High Spy.

At the very end of the film, after the final twist, Samantha attempts to

Grange Bridge in Borrowdale.

find some tranquil sublimity atop the place Ian had tried to take her to before. Here, the cameras pan-out revealing one of the most spectacular views in the Lake District from Fleetwith's lower summit, Honister Crag. Casting a stately presence over Buttermere and the Honister pass (B5289) the awe-inspiring panorama affords a fine prospect of two other lakes, Crummock Water and Loweswater. Whilst the stately Pillar Mountain and Great Gable hold court in close attendance.

Honister Crag, CA12 5XJ. OS ref: NY 20500 14100.
Grange-in- Borrowdale, CA12 5UQ. OS ref: NY 25200 17500.

J

Julia
Fred Zinnemann, 1977
'Through it all friendship prevailed'

Certificate: 15 Colour: 117 minutes
Producers: Julien Derode (executive), Tom Pevsner (associate), Richard Roth
Screenplay: Alvin Sargent Photography: Douglas Slocombe
Music: Georges Delerue
Cast: Jane Fonda, Vanessa Redgrave, Meryl Streep

Principal photography began on the Norfolk coast at Winterton-on-Sea for legendary director Fred Zinnemann's penultimate production. After five days shooting on a vast stretch of sand dunes they eventually moved up to the North Lakes in Cumbria for two weeks. Here, the cast and crew stayed in twelve hotels and guesthouses dotted around Keswick, with production offices based at the beautiful Keswick Country House Hotel. This delightful construction had been originally built by the Cockermouth, Keswick and Penrith Railway Company to coincide with the building of a railway designed to transport iron ore from the West Cumbrian coast. The hotel opened in 1869 as the Lake District became more accessible for tourists and day-trippers. However, just over a century later in 1972, the line was closed. These days it still remains a popular walk out of town towards the small village of Threlkeld for visitors and locals alike. Despite unfavourable weather conditions, filming was completed on schedule and the production moved on to Oxford, before interior scenes were shot near the heart of London at Elstree and Shepperton Studios.

The film portrays the unique story of a famed Hollywood screen writer/playwright and a shady leader of a radical European anti-fascist movement. Based on a fabricated chapter from the late playwright Lillian Hellman's memoir *Pentimento*, it still continues to raise issues over the identity of who the real Julia might be. The film's opening and closing scenes were shot on Derwentwater, as Lillian sits fishing in a rowing boat, whilst her narration introduces the story.

Using the innovative editing style of Walter Murch (winner of three Academy Awards including *The English Patient* and *Apocalypse Now*), the film features a non-chronological narrative amid flashbacks of memory, fused

Derwentwater and Friar's Crag

together seamlessly by Douglas Slocombe's exquisite cinematography.

An impressive cast included an Oscar nomination for Hollywood megastar Jane Fonda as Lillian, and a best supporting actress award for British actress Vanessa Redgrave for the part of Julia. At the Academy Awards ceremony the outspoken Redgrave famously courted a great deal of controversy by delivering a typically passionate acceptance speech. Earlier, she had been forced to enter the building through a back entrance due to a number of staged protests from Jewish support groups. Many of who had also burnt effigies of Redgrave in protest of her public condemnations of Zionism. Despite all the animosity, she labelled her antagonists 'Zionist hoodlums' whilst collecting the award, to the visible shock of the audience.

The film did go on to become a huge international success, and was nominated for a total of eleven Academy Awards, winning in three categories. Including another best supporting actor triumph for a commanding performance by the well-respected Jason Robards (*All the President's Men*) as Lillian's mentor and part-time lover, Dashiell Hammett. It also marked the onscreen debut of triple Oscar winner, Meryl Streep at a surprisingly late 28 years of age.

Derwentwater, CA12 5UB. OS ref: NY 25992 21055.
Keswick Country House Hotel, CA12 4NQ. OS ref: NY 27092 23766.

K

Ken Russell's films

Gothic   1986
Certificate: 18   Colour: 87 minutes
Producers: Al Clark (executive), Penny Corke, Robert Devereux (executive), Robert Fox (uncredited)
Screenplay: Stephen Volk   Photography: Mike Southon
Music: Thomas Dolby
Cast: Gabriel Byrne, Julian Sands, Natasha Richardson

Mahler   1974
Certificate: 15   Colour: 115 minutes
Producers: Roy Baird, Sanford Lieberson (executive), David Puttnam (executive)
Screenplay: Ken Russell   Photography: Dick Bush
Cast: Robert Powell, Georgina Hale

The Rainbow   1989
Certificate: 15   Colour: 113 minutes
Producers: Dan Ireland (executive), William J. Quigley (executive), Ken Russell, Ronaldo Vasconcellos (line), Jeremy Bolt (assistant, uncredited)
Screenplay: Ken Russell, Vivian Russell
Photography: Billy Williams   Music: Carl Davis
Cast: Sammi Davis, Paul McGann, Amanda Donohoe

Tommy   1975
Certificate: 15   Colour: 111 minutes
Producers: Harry Benn (associate), Ken Russell, Christopher Stamp (executive), Robert Stigwood, Beryl Vertue (executive)
Screenplay: Ken Russell, Pete Townshend (rock opera)
Photography: Dick Bush, Ronnie Taylor
Cast: Roger Daltrey, Ann-Margret, Oliver Reed

He once labelled himself the 'Enfant terrible of British Cinema' during an autobiographical documentary filmed for a South Bank Show aired on TV in 1989. Yet, few could argue (since he passed away aged 84 in 2011), how much the flamboyant and provocative film director from Southampton had done towards putting the Lake District on the film map. Writing in his autobiography, *A British Picture* he recalled setting off to visit the Lake District for the first time (at nearly 40 years of age) to research locations for his 1967

Mahler – Robert Powell and Antonia Ellis at Castle Crag,
© *Photos 12/Alamy stock photograph.*

TV movie, *Dante's Inferno*.

It proved to be a journey that would change his life forever. Arriving in the area under the cover of darkness after spending nearly the entire day driving to his destination, he took an upstairs room at the former Lodore Swiss Hotel (now the Lodore Falls Hotel). Awaking to sunshine and the sound of birdsong, it was the vision when he parted the curtains that would go on to have such an overwhelming effect on the rest of his life. For immediately in front of him was the magnificent view across Derwentwater to the Skiddaw mountain range. With heart pounding and hair stood on end, he eventually described the moment as 'a vision of God'.

In that one freeze-frame he instantly fell head over heels with a landscape he termed 'magical' and quickly resolved to spend as much time as possible in the new Promised Land. What followed were a number of films using the Lake District as a stand-in for countries like Iceland, Norway, France or Bavaria; and if possible, the might of Skiddaw's splendour was to be captured on celluloid at every opportunity. Using the nineteenth century cottage he bought with his second wife Vivian in Borrowdale as a base, the sight of film crews traipsing through the valley became a common sight to both locals and tourists, many were even recruited as extras. The steep slopes of the Wastwater screes featured in the first motion picture he filmed in the area, during a quiet interlude spliced in-between a pivotal orgy scene from the most controversial film in his entire oeuvre, *The Devils* (1971).

Father Urbain Grandier (Oliver Reed) holds a piece of bread up to the scree fragments, whilst performing a communion service, kneeling beside England's deepest lake. A couple of years later in 1974 he returned to shoot around the shores of Derwentwater, for the fictionalised biographical film *Mahler,* based on the life of the Austrian composer. In the film's apocalyptic opening, the musician's wooden lakeside hut bursts into flames against the distinctive outline of Cat Bells, one of Lakeland's most popular climbs. Robert Powell played the neurotic composer in the first of two major roles under Russell's direction, whilst Georgina Hale (who also featured prominently in *The Devils*) won a BAFTA as his neglected wife Alma. The film also marked the first of a series of projects for Goodtimes Enterprises; the British production company run by David Puttnam and silent partner Sanford Lieberson.

Originally the plan had been to shoot in Bavaria, but when the company's German backers pulled out at the last minute, Puttnam suggested moving the production to Russell's adopted home at Keswick. This led to one of the film's most notorious sequences entitled 'The Convert, Starring Cosima Wagner (Antonia Ellis) with Gustav Mahler' being filmed at Castle Crag, a Lake District landmark, just up the road from Russell's home in Borrowdale.

A slapstick scene lasts for nearly eight minutes and involves Mahler forging a Nazi sword from the Jewish Star of David, set to the Burlesque movement from the composer's Ninth Symphony. Another scene filmed on Derwentwater sees a young Gustav (Gary Rich) nearly drowning whilst trying to impress his anti-Semitic schoolmates, in a sequence that Rich found

Dalt Wood, Borrowdale in Tommy © 1975 Columbia Pictures.

particularly uncomfortable, as he couldn't swim in real life.

A year later Russell was back filming in the same area again, when he opened the musical film of The Who's 1969 rock opera *Tommy* with a shot of the sun disappearing behind Captain Walker's (Robert Powell) head on a mountain top (presumably supposed to represent the god-like Skiddaw). However, the Captain moves just a few paces away from the sunset to join his wife Nora (Ann-Margret) for a cup of tea on top of Walla Crag, a 1,243ft hill near Keswick. The panoramic view in the background is a familiar one, across Derwentwater to the outline of Cat Bells and Maiden Moor that feature so prominently in many films shot in the Lake District. Next we see the pair frolicking under the Lodore Falls in Borrowdale, where Tommy is conceived.

The all-star cast also included Jack Nicholson as The Specialist and Paul Nicholas as Cousin Kevin, along with a number of rock stars, including The Who's singer Roger Daltry in the lead role of Tommy, Tina Turner as the Acid Queen, Eric Clapton as The Preacher, and Elton John as a skyscraper Doc Marten wearing Pinball maestro. Russell added his stalwart Oliver Reed to the cast in the role of Frank Hobbes, Tommy's evil step-dad. After starring in *The Devils*, Reed wasted no time in gaining a reputation as a hard drinking, wild-man, prone to spending the odd night in the cells. Intriguingly, his own nickname for Russell was Jesus! Towards the end of the film a gang of Hells Angels are embroiled in a fight scene filmed near Castle Crag at Dalt Wood quarry in Borrowdale. When the fighting's over they casually sit down to a fry-up.

After hand-gliding over the Borrowdale valley, Tommy seeks redemption at the place of his creation with a swim in the Lodore Falls. Next we see him climbing up the rocky face of Honister crag on Fleetwith Pike in order to welcome a sunrise with open arms. It is the same mythical mountain top that starts off the film.

Just over ten years later, Russell returned from a spell in Hollywood to film in the Lake District again, using the lakes and mountain scenery to stand-in for Switzerland during *Gothic* (1986). Budget restraints played a major part in this decision, but nevertheless he was still happy to film in an area he loved. The story recounts the night of horror when Mary Shelley created the infamous gothic tale of *Frankenstein* at Lord Byron's handsome lakeshore retreat. Natasha Richardson (daughter of Vanessa Redgrave, who played Sister Jeanne in *The Devils*) played Mary. However, the Cumbrian weather didn't play ball, as the crew grappled with one of the worst summers on record. Unfortunately, roaring gales and bouts of heavy mist simply obscured the hills.

Russell later conceded they could've filmed in Hyde Park on the banks of the Serpentine for the same results, but a lot cheaper. Despite the hazardous conditions he did get to film one memorable scene on the banks of Derwentwater. In his autobiography he had indicated upon his death that he wanted a funeral pyre set up there, with his ashes then scattered over his beloved Skid-

Dalt Wood, Borrowdale – the deserted quarry today.

daw. At the end of *Gothic*, he got to stage a dress rehearsal, as a big pyre containing the drowned Romantic poet Percy Bysshe Shelley (Julian Sands) was constructed on the exact spot he had in mind. It was then set aflame on the exposed shoreline south of Calf Close Bay, looking back towards Skiddaw. In the very last scene a distinctive Lakeland steamer makes an appearance on the choppy waters of Ullswater, whilst a tour guide relates the tragic outcome of Mary Shelley's life to a bunch of drenched tourists.

There would be more wrangling over the size of budget involved with his next major film, an adaptation of D. H. Lawrence's *The Rainbow* (1989) written by Russell and his wife. During negotiations with his producer, Ronaldo Vasconcellos, the production company Vestron Pictures instructed Russell to lose half a million pounds from the estimated £2.5 million budget. Regrettably, this led to them deciding to shoot the film around the London area and not the Lake District as originally planned. They did however; still manage to shoot a few scenes in Cumbria. The sensuous film that eventually emerged was a prequel to the Oscar winning *Women in Love* (1969) and starred Sammi Davis as Ursula Brangwen, a young girl trying to discover her sexuality. Davis won the part for her performance as Mary Trent in Russell's comedy horror based on a Bram Stoker novel, *The Lair of the White Worm* released the previous year.

Amanda Donohoe who had played Lady Sylvia Marsh (the Snake

Woman) in the same film, also returned in *The Rainbow* as gym mistress Winifred Inger, who enjoys a passionate affair with Ursula at school. In one of only a handful of Lake District scenes, they go for a walk over the well-known summit of Helm Crag overlooking Grasmere in the central Lakes. Beside its distinctive 'Lion and Lamb' shaped rocks they meet an artist called Mack played by the eccentric English actor Dudley Sutton, who also featured as Baron de Laubardemont in *The Devils*. Ursula goes on to marry the soldier Anton Skrebensky played by Paul McGann, the co-star of another Cumbrian classic, *Withnail and I*.

Russell returned back full circle to the place where it all began for him, when he shot Skrebensky and Ursula's infamous love scene beside the cascading Lodore Falls.

Killer's Moon Alan Birkinshaw, 1978

'Nine attractive girls... Four dangerous men... One Endless Night of Terror!'

Certificate: 18
Producers: Alan Birkinshaw, Gordon Keymer.
Photography: Arthur Lavis
Music: John Shakespeare, Derek Warne
Cast: Anthony Forrest, Tom Marshall, Georgina Kean

Colour, 90 minutes
Screenplay: Alan Birkinshaw

As night-time approaches, a coach carrying a choir of teenage schoolgirls breaks down in a peaceful part of the Lake District. The girls are forced to abandon the bus and take shelter, eventually finding some in an isolated hotel closed for the winter. At the exact same time, four mentally ill patients escape from a nearby cottage hospital. Each one of them has been put on a special course of LSD mixed with dream therapy as part of a bizarre treatment to 'cure' them. Believing they are in some form of fantasy, the men are free to roam the moonlit landscape at will – you can probably guess the rest...

Oh, and the dangerous quartet are all dressed in the same kind of white outfits and bowler hats worn by young Alex and his fellow Droogs in Stanley Kubrick's notorious ultra-violent film, *A Clockwork Orange*. And the plot of *Killer's Moon* tries to follow a similar path, as the loonies murder the coach driver, a gamekeeper and his wife, before making their way towards an inevitable rendezvous with the schoolgirls. Who are of course completely unaware of their imminent danger, and remain holed-up at an isolated country house clutching teddies dressed in their nightdresses.

Displaying the Lake District as a backdrop throughout, Director Alan Birkinshaw used Armathwaite Hall near Bassenthwaite Lake as the hotel where the girls endure an ordeal at the hands of the drugged-up tormentors.

Armathwaite Hall Country House Hotel, Bassenthwaite Lake, Keswick, ©Armathwaite Hall.

Originally one of England's stately homes, today the mansion is a luxury 4 star hotel, in the private hands of the Graves family for nearly 40 years. Built in the eleventh century, guests have included members of the aristocracy, parliament and ironically during the Second World War a group of girls from Hunmanby Gap school were evacuated to stay at the hall. However, as in *Killer's Moon*, it seems not much study took place during that particular episode, according to the girls' own admissions afterwards! Set in some 400 acres of deer park and woodland, with outstanding views of the magnificent Skiddaw mountain range, it's easy to see why the eminent novelist Sir Hugh Walpole once described the mansion as 'A house of perfect and irresistible charm.'

The film's director Alan Birkinshaw once tellingly advised viewers, 'not to take the film too seriously!' before a screening at the Ten Years of Terror-film convention held in London, 2001. Perhaps audiences should have known what to expect given that his first film offering in 1974 *Confessions of a Sex Maniac* had been a send-up about a young architect whose dream was to build an office block in the shape of a breast! It starred the late Roger Lloyd Pack, who went on to play Trigger in *Only Fools and Horses* and was even dubbed 'poorly made cat litter' on the video's promotional sleeve.

It's fair to say *Killer's Moon* has consistently divided opinion into two groups since the late 1970s. Namely those believing it a genuine cult movie or those convinced it is just misconceived trash. It's also intriguing to note that it was bracketed as a 'video nasty' and awarded an X certificate upon its original release, especially considering the comedic level of sex and violence by today's standards. In fact, viewing the film over 30 years on you seriously wonder how anyone could've been vaguely frightened by it, given the appalling level of acting and tasteless dialogue, not to mention a cheesy, soft-porn soundtrack. But perhaps Birkinshaw was just having a laugh at everyone's expense, and this is actually a comedy, subverting exploitation movies from within. After all, can you really take a film seriously that contains a three-legged dog, a Government minister who dreams of murder, rape, and pillage, a soundtrack featuring 'Three blind mice' played (very badly) on a Bontempi organ, and dialogue such as: 'Look, you were only raped. As long as you don't tell anyone about it you'll be alright!'

Armathwaite Hall, Bassenthwaite, CA12 4RE. OS ref: NY 20633 32466.

Killing Me Softly Chen Kaige, 2002
'What if your desires unlocked hidden secrets?'

Certificate: 18   Colour: 100 minutes
Producers: Anna Chi (associate), Michael Chinich, Daniel Goldberg (executive), Donna Grey (line), Joe Medjuck, Lynda Myles, Tom Pollock (executive), Ivan Reitman (executive)
Screenplay: Kara Lindstrom   Photography: Arthur Lavis
Music: Patrick Doyle
Cast: Heather Graham, Joseph Fiennes, Natascha McElhone

Matterdale church located to the north-west of Ullswater, features prominently in Chinese director Chen Kaige's first and only English language film to date. Touted as an erotic thriller, it starred Heather Graham (*Boogie Nights*) as Alice Loudon, and Joseph Fiennes (*Shakespeare in Love*) who plays Adam Tallis, a famous mountaineer with a murky past. Adapted from the 1999 book of the same name by the best-selling crime writing partnership of Nicci French (a pseudonym for married couple Nicci Gerrard and Sean French) the film however, was released to mixed reviews.

Montecito Pictures a production company formed by Ivan Reitman (director of *Ghostbusters*) and Tom Pollock (an ex-chairman of Universal Pictures) snapped up the film rights after the authors had barely delivered the manuscript to their publishers. It didn't take long before a script was hastily written, although it contained a crucial change that did not meet with the author's approval. Ironically, whilst researching the novel, an ill prepared French and Gerrard went walking in the Lake District on what appeared to be a sunny day, until the unpredictable Cumbrian weather closed in on them.

Fog quickly descended on the fells and they were grateful to be led to safety by another group of walkers who baulked at their shabby trainers and lack of waterproofs, gloves or hats.

In the film version, Alice bumps into Adam at a set of traffic lights on a London Street and falls immediately in love with his rugged athleticism. Within days they are hastily married. The steamy action moves swiftly away from the crowded city streets to the open countryside of the Lake District landscape. Here the couple are first glimpsed encountering the sharp twists and turns of the Kirkstone Pass in a small sports car. Their wedding ceremony takes place inside the old Matterdale church, before Alice completely strips off her all-in-one bridal dress beside a grave just outside, to be photographed in the buff by her new husband! The gloves and the rest of the kit are definitely off for the honeymoon…

Dating from late Elizabethan times, the grade II listed stone and slate chapel was originally part of the parish of Greystoke. Local tradition dictates the church to have been hallowed by the reading of the word and years of prayer from the faithful, after being built without a formal dedication, a common feature in many old chapelries. Today, two other items of note inside the church include: a knob on the pulpit which came from a preacher's black gown and the wide bench beside the door that was originally used to rest coffins on before burials.

Not long into their marriage, Adam's shady past becomes a major headache to Alice when she begins to receive anonymous letters full of warnings about her betrothed. Discovering a previous girlfriend died whilst climbing with him, she soon begins to wonder whom she has got involved with.

Matterdale Church, Greystoke, Ullswater.

The film's climax takes place back at the old church again, where Alice and Adam's sister Deborah, played by Natascha McElhone (*The Truman Show*) look for the remains of the disappeared girlfriend. A showdown ensues, after Alice discovers the hole they are both digging is intended for her to be buried in. Fortunately, Adam arrives just in the nick of time to rescue his confused wife from the clutches of a psychotic, jealous sister.

Greystoke, near Ullswater, CA11 0TP. OS ref: NY 44039 30777.

L

Lakeland Rock Paul Berriff, 1985

'To extend the limits of what had previously seemed impossible'

Television film and DVD
Format: PAL
Manufacturer: Striding Edge
Colour: 98 minutes
Region code: Region 2

'It all began right here on these crags, high above Wasdale, one of the most beautiful valleys in the English Lake District.'

So begins one of Britain's leading mountaineers Sir Chris Bonington, in his introduction to a classic rock climbing film. Previously only available on video, *Lakeland Rock* was finally made available on DVD by Striding Edge back in 2005. This inspirational film features five major climbs in the Lake District, each one considered to be a major step forward in the exhilarating sport. Director Paul Berriff puts the camera crew right in the middle of the action throughout with a series of radical sound and camera techniques, adding a touch of genuine drama and tension on all the climbs.

During the film they re-enact some of the old methods used, often showing the strain and sheer physical exertion required to complete unbelievably steep climbs. It is all beautifully contrasted against some terrific footage of the surrounding Lakeland landscape. First broadcast by Channel Four in 1985, it includes Sir Chris climbing with three significant first ascenders. Eagle Front ('Climbing with Mackerel on your feet') is now seen as a fitting testimonial to one of the great Cumbrian pioneers, Bill Peascod, who sadly died just after filming his classic route (successfully completed back in 1941) on Eagle Crag, Buttermere.

Another tribute sees Bonington climbing Dovedale Groove ('climbing like a ruptured duck') with the late Don Whillans who became one of the world's greatest mountaineers. Despite an obvious depreciation of his former powers and not to mention bulging wasteline, Whillans hauls himself up the imposing scramble on lonely Dove Crag, Dovedale, reputedly one of the most impressive pieces of all Lakeland rock. A colourful ex-plumber from Manchester, Whillans had first climbed it back in May 1954 with Joe Brown and Don Cowan. Unfortunately, he turned to drink in his later years and regrettably died of a heart attack in his sleep at just 52 years of age, not long after filming with Bonington.

In the last climb, Bonington himself gets into all sorts of bother on the crux move of Footless Crow, Goat Crag in Borrowdale. First climbed in 1976 by Pete Livesey, it became regarded as one of his defining masterpieces. These days it is seen as a quantum leap in difficulty, particularly for the way it changed the sport and ushered in a new breed of climber. Watching Bonington struggle so much whilst openly despairing about a slack rope proves to be quite uncomfortable viewing!

The final two films showcase the skills of Gill Price and Jill Lawrence, two leading women climbers who make light work of Empire on Raven Crag, above Thirlmere in the central fells.

Raven Crag, Thirlmere.

Whilst Pete Whillance and Dave Armstrong add a stunning finale to the film by ascending Incantations on Tophet Wall, Wasdale – unofficially, labelled the birthplace of rock climbing. At the time of filming this was the toughest route climbed in the Lake District, and is still rated as 'hard severe.'

Although nearly 30 years old, this vintage film of rock climbing history is still hugely riveting, as it not only marks the final contributions of two of the sports' most valued trailblazers, but also retains a sense of authentic truth, that continues to help make it accessible both to climbers and anyone with a general curiosity about the Lake District.

Eagle Crag, Buttermere, CA13 9UY. OS ref: NY 17700 20500.
Dove Crag, Dovedale, CA11 0NZ. OS ref: NY 37500 10900.

Goat Crag, Borrowdale, CA12 5XA. OS ref: NY 24500 16400.
Raven Crag, Thirlmere, CA12 4TG. OS ref: NY 30400 18700.
Tophet Wall, Wasdale, CA12 5XJ. OS ref: NY 21000 10000.

Let Sleeping Corpses Lie

Jorge Grau, 1974

'One of the best zombie films ever made!'

Certificate: 18
Colour: 95 minutes
Producers: Edmondo Amati, Manuel Pérez
Screenplay: Sandro Continenza, Marcello Coscia
Music: Giuliano Sorgini
Cast: Cristina Galbó, Ray Lovelock, Arthur Kennedy

Two young strangers meet each other in peculiar circumstances at a petrol station while visiting the Lake District. As fate continually conspires against them, an embittered local police chief (Arthur Kennedy – *Lawrence of Arabia*) begins to suspect the pair of committing a series of Satanist murders; yet unbeknown to him, the real culprits are the living dead, brought to life by an agricultural machine that kills microbes through ultrasound.

The film is Spanish Director Jorge Grau's take on the George Romero classic *Night of the Living Dead* and has become something of a hidden gem for fans of zombie horror. Incredibly, it was released under sixteen different titles internationally, including: *Don't Open the Window* or *The Living Dead at Manchester Morgue*. The film followed immediately after his equally gruesome creation *Ceremonia Sangrienta (Bloody Ceremony)*, similarly put out under numerous guises in 1973. Both films were made with a Spanish/Italian co-production, thanks to the continued perseverance of Edmondo Amanti, who'd initially touted the idea of making a colour homage of Romero's black and white masterpiece a few years before.

Curiously, the film's locations include: Derbyshire, Cheshire and Rome, while the opening scenes unfold in a much altered Manchester city centre, before the arrival of the Arndale Shopping Centre. Many of these locations were blown away by an IRA bomb blast in 1996, which devastated large sections of the northern parts of the city and led to a partial rebuilding of the Arndale centre. A couple of scenes were filmed on the outskirts of the Lake District when antique dealer George (Ray Lovelock – *Fiddler on the Roof*) rides his gruff sounding Norton motorbike through Manchester before stopping at a Fina garage just off the A590 close to Levens in the South Lakes.

It is here in the film that Edna (Cristina Galbó) accidently backs into George's bike, forcing him to leave it for repair. After a brief exchange they

The garage on the A5074 Lyth Valley road.

both end up setting off in her Mini down the A5074 Lyth Valley Road towards a rendezvous with their impending doom.
Levens, LA8 8EL. OS ref: SD 47301 85451.

Life of a Mountain: Scafell Pike

Terry Abraham, 2014

'A Year in the Life of England's Highest Peak'

DVD
Format: PAL
Music: Freddie Hongoler

Colour: 125 minutes
Region code: All regions
Manufacturer: Striding Edge

Critically acclaimed independent film-maker Terry Abraham's homage to the highest peak in England became the realisation of a long held ambition in 2014. Inspiration for capturing the rugged mountain at Wasdale's heart had originally developed over many years spent walking and backpacking in the western Lake District. As a youngster, Abraham made his first visit to the area aged thirteen, when he first set eyes on the deep romantic chasms and characteristic beauty that would go on to resonate with him on such a profound level.

A few years later in his mid-twenties, wild camping in all seasons and weather conditions started to become an obsession. Crucially, these trips also afforded him enough time to witness and appreciate some of the more extraordinary sights away from the main paths to the summits. Absorbing awe-inspiring visual feasts, coupled with the social history of the area, has undoubtedly helped shape Abraham's subsequent movies. After beginning to work with film in his spare time it didn't take long before he sought to bring his own unique vision and passion for the Lakeland fells like no other before him. Opportunity knocked after he was made redundant, when he decided to dedicate himself exclusively to filming.

Clearly a labour of love for a relative unknown with no formal training, the sheer scale of the Scafell project almost threatened to overwhelm him both physically and mentally. There was also the considerable task of raising enough funds to enable him to live in the area over an 18-month period. In the end this was achieved thanks mainly to the efforts of a large community of followers and sponsors on the world's largest fund raising website 'Indiegogo', who made substantial financial contributions to the project. Soon enough, the Wasdale fells became a home from home, as the Nottinghamshire based filmmaker set about recounting the changing seasons throughout a year of the infamous mountain region. The results are certainly a remarkable achievement considering it was only his second production (the first film, *The Cairngorms in Winter,* with Chris Townsend, had been released on DVD a year earlier in 2013).

Rather unnervingly, he only completed filming the final scenes of the Scafell film just a couple of weeks before its premiere in May 2014 at the impressive IMAX screen at Rheged Centre (near Penrith). A special hour long edited version also debuted on BBC Four during January 2015.

The film has since become renowned for a number of rarely seen spectacular night-time images that were painstakingly captured using time-lapse photography. Another predominant feature of the film is all the unscripted contributions from both well-known locals who work in the area and those who choose to visit. Almost exclusively a one-man band, Abraham frequently headed off unaided into the clouds, weighed-down with all sorts of equipment. The tremendous effort involved in carrying his paraphernalia meant he felt more like a packhorse than a film-maker at times. Many unrelenting hours spent plodding up and down the Scafells, often with a rucksack weighing in excess of 30 kilos, armed with a few days' food, camping equipment and video gear, made the considerable task seem brutal at times.

A lengthy equipment list included: two cameras (one for time-lapse and photography, the other for video) with countless memory cards and batteries, chargers and leads, tripods, a mini-crane and much more during days and nights out under the stars. Signature features of Abraham's films to date are the meditative cycles of spectacular sunsets and sunrises, sweeping panoramas and time-lapsed shots, (first glimpsed to such magnificent effect in the *Cairngorms in Winter*).

Yet *Life of a Mountain* is also the story of the people who live, work and care for the iconic fells. Alison O'Neill is the first local face to appear in her guise as 'the Barefoot Shepherdess' dressed in a trademark tweed skirt. O'Neill is well known for displaying many different talents. These range predominantly from farming sheep in the Howgills (near Sedbergh), or in other roles such as a qualified walk guide, fashion designer, sometime poet and proud Cumbrian. A self-confessed romantic, she strides through the landscape mirroring the celebrated literary figures of 200 years past, speaking passionately about the importance of maintaining local traditions. She memorably describes the mountain as 'a huge stairway to heaven made of rock'.

One of the first to climb its rocky pleasure domes was the Romantic poet Samuel Taylor Coleridge, who famously wrote the first ever 'Scafell letter' to Sara Hutchinson (a member of Wordsworth's intimate circle) on the summit in August 1802. Abraham references Coleridge's early exploits along with the climbing associations at Wasdale, when filming Alan Hinkes (a veteran Himalayan mountaineer) exploring the deep gully leading down to Mickledore, known as 'Fat Man's Agony'. Sensibly, Hinkes declines to climb down from the notorious Mountain Rescue black spot, 'Broad Stand' in typically slippery and dangerous conditions. Coleridge had experienced similar problems when confronted with the steep drop down from the rocky ledge, but feeling overawed by the impetuous clouds, attempted what the Fell and Rock Club now consider to be England's first recreational rock climb. Coleridge got lucky, many are not.

There are other appearances from television regulars such as David Powell-Thompson who assisted Julia Bradbury on the BBC's *Wainwright Walks* series. Wainwright famously devoted 28 pages to the mountain in his pictorial guides. He declared Piers Ghyll, an old haunt for botanists searching for plants in the dank and dark crevices as his favourite route to the top. Continuing with the Wainwright connections, A.W.'s old sparring partner from the original BBC series: writer, broadcaster and Chairman of the Wainwright Society, Eric Robson appears briefly at the Wasdale Shepherd's meet, whilst Mark Richards (author of the *Lakeland Fellranger* series of guide books and another good friend to A.W.) also contributes.

In a rare interview, local sheep farmer and celebrated fell runner 'Iron' Joss Naylor MBE discusses the tradition and craft of building a dry stonewall. Naylor, who was born and bred at Wasdale Head and has lived in the region for nearly 80 years also nonchalantly mentions how he once ran from Wasdale to the summit cairn and back again in an incredible 47 minutes! Abraham assembled an impressive cast of locals relatively easily after approaching them individually to talk about the project. As filming progressed, they warmly accepted him into the heart of the community. The film also provides a number

Abraham's signature time-lapse footage over the Scafells,
© Terry Abraham.

of fascinating insights into the area's day-to-day life with contributions from all sorts of people. Be it from fell-walkers and tourists, there are differing points of view surrounding the Three Peaks Challengers or the trials and tribulations of National Trust rangers and local farmers.

Incredibly, as Abraham does not drive, he had to rely upon either public transport or Powell-Thompson collecting him by car from the train to reach the Wasdale valley. From here he would set off on foot up onto the fells. Filming on the north or south side of the Scafells depended on the time of year and where the sun would rise and set. He soon discovered how the sun set in perfect alignment with Eskdale during the late autumn to early spring period, casting a magical light onto the wild side of Scafell Pike. As a result, Abraham seldom camped in the same place twice, preferring to just go with the flow, filming the mountain either close up or from a distance in order to capture all of its facets. However, the high craggy tops of the old Roman fort at Hard Knott became one of his favourite vantage points in clear autumnal skies.

Having originally planned to make a series of three films on the highest peaks of mainland Britain (Ben Nevis, Snowdon and Scafell Pike) he chose instead to produce a sequel to the Scafell film, as *Life of a Mountain: Blencathra* premiered at Rheged in May 2016. Other collaborations with renowned wild camper and author Chris Townsend came out in 2014 with *Backpacking in the Lake District* and *The Lake District: Helvellyn* with Mark Richards, both released through Striding Edge on DVD.

He filmed Townsend, (a stalwart in most of his productions so far), wild camping at Great Moss in the Scafell film. Despite receiving many plaudits for his efforts, including an award for excellence from the Outdoor Writers and Photographers Guild, Abraham still prefers to label himself a backpacker above either a film-maker or photographer. Yet with the promise of more dramatic and remarkable footage on the roof of Britain's mountains to come, further recognition will undoubtedly follow.

Scafell Pike, CA20 1EX (nearest). OS ref: NY 21588 07185
Hardknott Pass, NY 222015.

The Loss of Sexual Innocence

Mike Figgis, 1999

'A film that examines the way Sex, Guilt and Knowledge interact'

Certificate: 18 Colour: 106 minutes
Producers: Mike Figgis, Barney Reisz, Annie Stewart, Patrick Wachsberger
Screenplay: Mike Figgis Photography: Benôit Delhomme
Cast: Julian Sands, Saffron Burrows Music: Mike Figgis

Carlisle features heavily in a frequently hard to fathom film, written and directed by Mike Figgis (*Leaving Las Vegas*), who was born in Cumbria's county town in 1948. Returning to his childhood roots, he filmed scenes at Denton Holme and Dixon's chimney at Shaddon Mill in the historic city. Built by its first owner Peter Dixon in 1835-6, the mill is situated on the boundary of the inner-city district of Denton Holme and Caldewgate, where the large chimney used to be one of the tallest in the UK.

This renowned landmark structure (known as 'Dixon's Chimney' after its founder) is now only just short of its original height after a recent restoration. The film came four years after Figgis's Oscar nominations for Best Director and Best Adapted Screenplay on the surprise hit *Leaving Las Vegas* and demonstrated a return to low-budget, so called art-house film-making. It traces the story of a young boy called Nic at various stages of his life.

His tale is interspersed with the story of Adam and Eve in an experimental, non-linear semi-autobiographical visual mood-piece. Figgis enjoyed a different upbringing to most children when he moved abroad with his family to colonial Kenya's capital Nairobi, until returning back to the UK to settle in a very working-class area of Newcastle when just eight years old. Initially titled *Short Stories*, a relatively short 60-page script had been penned in the early 1980s, taking its inspiration from Ernest Hemingway's *Nick Adams Stories*, a collection of both well known and unknown works republished

Standing tall, Dixon's Chimney, Carlisle.

posthumously in 1972.

Intriguingly, Figgis's mother had worked for Hemingway whilst the family were living in Nairobi, typing up an article her son's favourite writer had been commissioned to write on Africa for *Look* magazine. The theme of secret desires is introduced early on in the film when a young Nic (aged five) observes an old man watching a young African girl reading from the bible, dressed revealingly in torn lingerie. Ten years later, Jonathan Rhys Meyers plays a teenage Nic, in his next role after playing Bruno in Michael Radford's *B. Monkey*. He gets ignored by his drunken girlfriend Susan (Kelly MacDonald – *Trainspotting*) at a family function; eventually finding her kissing an older man in an upstairs bedroom. Julian Sands (*Gothic*) plays the adult Nic; a film director stuck in a sexually frustrated marriage. Throughout the film, Nic's loss of innocence is juxtaposed with the parable of Adam and Eve, with some fragmented dreamlike scenes from the bible story staged in a muddied lake, featuring an African Adam – Femi Ogumbanjo and a Scandinavian Eve – Hanne Klintoe. Ultimately 'their fall' becomes an allegory for the events unfolding in Nic's life.

Due to the project's dire financial plight, some African scenes were actually filmed near the border town of Morpeth in Northumberland. A truckload of red soil was purchased and poured all over the one remaining maize field in the area. They also hired a few Zimbabwean students who were studying nearby at Newcastle University as extras. Figgis often provided the soundtracks to many of his own films, after gaining experience in numerous bands during his formative years, including a stint playing trumpet and guitar in a band called 'Gas Board' with Bryan Ferry (pre-Roxy Music days) amongst others.

Throughout many of the film's sequences he skilfully weaves in pieces by Beethoven, Mozart, Chopin and Schumann. Filmed in just under a month and shot entirely on 16mm, the film has a pure, almost ethereal look throughout.

During the shoot, Figgis was dating British actress Saffron Burrows (*Deep Blue Sea*), who features as an Italian actress bizarrely coming face-to-face with her long-lost twin at an airport, in yet another random fragment. However, three years after the film's release, 29 year old Burrows split from a 53 year old Figgis after five years together. She kept media tongues wagging by immediately starting a relationship with Harry Potter's Mrs Dursley (Fiona Shaw) whom she starred with in Deborah Warner's adaptation of Jeanette Winterson's novel, *The PowerBook* at the National Theatre.

Denton Holme, Carlisle, CA2 5EL. OS ref: NY 39813 55218.

M

The Maniac Project

N. Andrew Elliot, 2010

'Sometimes one maniac is not enough'

Certificate: 18   Colour: 75 minutes
Producers: Jay Boryczko, N. Andrew Elliot, Darren Horne
Screenplay: Jay Boryczko, N. Andrew Elliot   Music: Antony Groves

A Cumbrian film attempted to put British B-movies back on the map in 2012, when a student project filmed purely for laughs, became a multi-award winning feature. This proved some achievement considering it had only cost the paltry sum of £500 to make! The filmmakers described their spoof horror as a '1970s grindhouse comedy action film' made in the style of 'King of the cult film' American director, Roger Corman (*Little Shop of Horrors*). The film was written and directed by Andrew Elliott and produced by Darren

There's a killer on the loose again! © Andrew Elliot

Horne, then manager of the Lonsdale Alhambra Cinema in Penrith. It took the pair three years to put together what they readily admit was ludicrous nonsense!

Shot entirely in Cumbria, locations included Elliott's house in Carlisle, various local fields and woodland nearby, the cinema in Penrith and Atlas House, a traditional brick and slate four storey former mill in the inner-city suburb of Denton Holme, Carlisle. The story is set in a land awash with murderous maniacs who become obsessed with filming their own battles. As each character's fame spreads, so their egos increase as they begin competing with one another to see who can become the biggest celebrity. A Wild-West slaughter-fest ensues, where the maniacs embark on a daily fight to the death. However, one of them, Mysterious Man, decides to turn the carnage into an entertainment opportunity by rounding up nine of the most notorious assassins in order to make the greatest exploitative, snuff movie ever made.

The film gained valuable recognition after being shown at film festivals in the US, winning the Award of Merit at the Accolade awards in California and the Indie Fest international competition. It is now available to be seen worldwide on iTunes, Netflix and more after being bought by the Los Angeles Company, New World Distribution. To celebrate the global digital distribution deal a special free screening of the film was held at the Alhambra, Penrith in September 2012.

Carlisle, CA2 5EL. OS ref: NY 39813 55218.
Alhambra Cinema, Penrith, CA11 7PT. OS ref: NY 51474 30311.

Miss Potter   Chris Noonan, 2006

'The life of Beatrix Potter is the most enchanting tale of all'

Certificate: PG   Colour: 88 minutes
Producers: David Kirschner, Mike Medavoy, Corey Sienega, David Thwaites
Screenplay: Richard Maltby Jr.   Photography: Andrew Dunn
Music: Nigel Westlake
Cast: Renée Zellweger, Ewan McGregor, Emily Lloyd

The 'Miss Potter effect', saw tourists start heading back to the Lake District in droves. The film's phenomenal success clearly helped heal any leftover trauma from the tragic foot and mouth outbreak that so beset the region at the start of the new millennium. With visitor figures to Hill Top (Beatrix's former Lakeland home) now consistently averaging around 100,000 per year, the film continues to be not only a wonderful showcase for Beatrix Potter, but for the Lake District as a whole.

It is intriguing to think that a biopic about the woman who helped preserve the area for what it is known for today, once again served to re-ignite and prompt a flood of people to return. None more so than the additional influx of visitors from Japan, who had already adopted Beatrix as one of their favourite authors, seeing as her hugely popular 23 little books were once a part of the school curriculum there.

However, getting *Miss Potter* to the screen proved to be a convoluted process, until it finally emerged after nearly fifteen years of tortuous wrangling. It all began when 67-year-old Richard Maltby, Jr wrote the film's screenplay back in 1992. Initially the script attracted interest from a number of producers, but it wasn't until David Kirschner and Corey Sienega came onboard that events finally started moving in the right direction. They gathered further impetus during a meeting between Maltby's agent and David Thwaites (a young British producer, representing former Phoenix Pictures studio chief Mike Medavoy) at the 2003 Sundance Film Festival – the home of Robert Redford's renamed Hollywood schmooze-a-thon since 1981, perched in a valley some 6,800 feet above the eastern Utah desert. (Incidentally, another film with a Cumbrian connection: Danny Boyle's zombie flick *28 Days Later* had its North American premiere at the festival that same year).

Arnold W. Messer (another key producer) got involved, as a deal was put together involving financing from Summit Entertainment, the UK Film Council's Premiere Fund, Grosvenor Park and the Isle of Man Film Commission. Momentum Pictures bought the UK and Spanish distribution rights, whilst the Weinstein Company purchased them in the US. Next up, a multi-award winning cast and crew were assembled, including the Australian director Chris Noonan, who had not actually directed a film since the surprise 1995 hit, *Babe,* the heart-warming story of a pig who learned how to herd sheep. The London-based Australian actress Cate Blanchett, who had first voiced an interest in playing the role of Beatrix, introduced Noonan to the project. Although Noonan had reservations that *Miss Potter* would be 'a cutesy kiddie story' he soon changed his mind when he read Maltby's script; likening it to the story of a modern woman plonked into the middle of Victorian England, having to contend with an incredibly restrictive society.

The intimidating task of playing Beatrix eventually fell to 37-year-old American actress, Renée Zellweger (*Bridget Jones's Diary*). Although initially appearing to be something of a surprise choice for such a well renowned character from British history, she pulled it off effortlessly. Recruiting the services of her trusted dialect coach Barbara Berkery, who'd previously helped her on both *Bridget Jones* films to great effect. Zellweger asserted her position as the film's executive producer by speaking directly with the illustrious Scottish actor, Ewan MacGregor (*Star Wars Episodes I-III*) convincing him to trade light-sabres for rabbits by taking on the role of Norman Warne, Beatrix's publisher and eventual fiancé. They had already developed consid-

Renée Zellweger as Miss Potter beside Derwentwater
© *AF archive/Alamy Stock Photo*

erable on-screen chemistry when co-starring in 2003's *Down with Love*, a colourful homage to the 1960s Doris Day and Rock Hudson romantic comedies.

Twice Oscar nominated British actress Emily Watson (*War Horse*), played Norman's sister, Millie; whilst seasoned professional Bill Paterson (*The Killing Fields*) was cast as Beatrix's father Rupert, opposite her incredibly snooty mother, Helen, recreated superbly by the well-respected television actress Barbara Flynn. A relative unknown Lloyd Owen (*Apollo 18*) became William Heelis, Beatrix's Lake District property advisor and future husband.

The bulk of the story is concerned with the early 1900s, where Beatrix is depicted as a strong-willed, unmarried 36-year-old woman, on the cusp of publishing her first 'bunny book', *The Tale of Peter Rabbit*. Together with Norman, they successfully oversee her initial publishing output, as she starts to become one of the most famous children's authors of all time, whilst their affections for each other grow at a similar pace. Soon they begin a love affair and become unofficially engaged, much against her parent's wishes. Ultimately it all ends abruptly with Norman's sudden death aged just 37 years old due to pernicious anaemia. This dangerous condition occurs when the body can't make enough healthy red blood cells because of a lack of vitamin B12 (these days it would be relatively easy to treat with vitamin pills.)

Beatrix tries to escape the pain of Norman's death by moving to the Lake District, where she buys Hill Top farm and opts to run it as a going concern. During this period she meets her prospective partner, William Heelis, a solicitor and land agent. William starts to advise her about the local farms that are being sold off to property developers. Finding this situation intolerable, Beatrix typically starts to intervene, buying up farms to both protect and prevent them from going to the developers. Thus, the story ends with the green shoots of what became the National Trust, as we know it today.

A number of scenic locations from around the Lake District were used in the film, with the rest of filming taking place in London, Middlesex, Kingston-upon-Thames, East Sussex and the Isle of Man. The decision to shoot some of the scenes in the Lake District proved essential for Chris Noonan, who insisted it would've been a travesty had they not filmed there. In the opening scene, Beatrix is seen sitting on the open fell-side, writing studiously on the pages of a book placed delicately on her lap, with a glorious view across Loweswater from Miresyke, looking towards Carling Knott opposite. Mellbreak lies directly to her left, with the farmhouse cleverly hidden just out of shot. It was not however, the original choice of location to open the film with. This had apparently been way over on the other side of the valley; yet due to the merciless Cumbrian weather on the morning of the last day of re-shoots, the production team had to move their equipment at the very last minute, to happen upon what would undoubtedly be the ideal spot and opening to the film.

Many scenes were shot in and around Derwentwater, which featured heavily in Beatrix's early life, where she spent nine summer holidays staying at a couple of grand country house estates with her family between 1895-1907. Lingholm and Fawe Park's gardens and surrounding landscape were depicted in a number of her subsequent publications, as she filled sketchbooks with material that would later be used in the tales of Peter Rabbit, Squirrel Nutkin,

Yew Tree Farm, Coniston.

Benjamin Bunny and Mrs Tiggy Winkle – a hedgehog washer-woman who lived at the back of Cat Bells, close to the Newlands Valley. Perhaps the most contentious issue surrounding the movie was the decision *not* to film any scenes at Hill Top, Beatrix's former home in Near Sawrey that she gifted to the National Trust after her death in 1943.

Many reasons were given for this, ranging from the potential loss of revenue incurred by the Trust (from closing the property), to the restrictive amount of space inside, where only two angles would have presented a decent 'frame' for filming.

Despite the best efforts of the producers to use Hill Top, a compromise was finally reached, when the location managers Martin Joy and Beverley Lamb found an alternative farm, on the outskirts of Coniston. One of fifteen Beatrix gifted to the National Trust after her death, Yew Tree Farm had also featured on film some sixty years previously in Hitchcock's *The Paradine Case*, but for *Miss Potter* it had to undergo a complete transformation. After a number of negotiations with the Trust, production designer Martin Childs and his team began work on the modifications just days before the full film crew arrived. To fully resemble Hill Top, the whitewashed front of the farmhouse had to be painted over with a greeny-grey colour; the lawn had to be dug up and planted with summer flowers, whilst a dry stonewall was built across the entire width of the site. Director of photography Andrew Dunn BSc used carefully chosen camera angles to expertly disguise how Yew Tree farm sits at the bottom of a valley, dwarfed by both Holme Fell and Yewdale Fell. Chris Noonan even got in on the act, insisting that the pigpen constructed opposite the farm be covered on one side, after his previous experience of working with pigs on *Babe*.

Another location used nearby was the enchanting Loughrigg Tarn, glimpsed at the very beginning and just after Beatrix walks contentedly around its surrounding track with Mr. Heelis at the end of the film.

Situated just north of Skelwith Bridge, it lies at the foot of Loughrigg Fell, one of the most easily accessible and popular spots in the central area. The tarn was famously referred to by Wordsworth as 'Diana's looking-glass, round clear and bright as heaven' in a letter to his patron Sir George Beaumont. The setting where Beatrix signs the contract to buy Hill Top at William Heelis's solicitors office, was filmed at 'The Rum Story, The Dark Spirit of Whitehaven', on Cumbria's west coast. An award winning visitor attraction, 'The Rum Story' depicts the Georgian streets, cellars and bonded warehouses of the Jefferson family business, at a time when the UK's rum trade focused on the port of Whitehaven.

The film was certainly not without its critics at the time of release, one famously dubbing it a 'twee, dull English Heritage film that will appeal neither to children nor discerning adults!' They also criticised Zellweger for a whimsical portrayal of Beatrix and cited the animated drawings as looking

Loughrigg Tarn and track where Beatrix and William take a stroll.

too 'Disney-esque'. Inevitably, there were a couple of inaccuracies in the screenplay. For instance, there is no evidence to suggest Beatrix knew William Heelis in her childhood; whilst for practical and artistic reasons she hears about Norman's death in the Lake District, rather than in North Wales (where she actually received the tragic news). However, the film certainly proved to be a massive box-office success with most discerning Potter-ites and the public as a whole, grossing nearly £1.5 million over the opening weekend in the UK alone.

The resurgence of visitor numbers to both Hill Top and the Beatrix Potter gallery in Hawkshead (formerly the real offices of her husband) are a continuing testament of how, despite all convention, she went on to achieve more in her lifetime (and beyond) than most men of her time.

July 28th, 2016, marked what would have been her 150th birthday. To honour this, and say thanks for her work, the National Trust held a series of special events, activities and exhibitions across the Lake District celebrating her enduring legacy. *Miss Potter*'s tenth anniversary was also included amongst a number of special anniversaries for Potter fans, allowing visitors a rare chance to experience the set of the film at Yew Tree Farm, Coniston (the surrogate Hill Top), while Sticklebarn, Great Langdale, held a special screening on the big day itself.

Miresyke, Loweswater, CA13 0SU. OS ref: NY 12220 22480.
Yew Tree Farm, Coniston, LA21 8DP. OS ref: SD 31939 99839.
The Rum Story, Whitehaven, CA28 7DN. OS ref: NX 97313 18125.
Fawe Park, Portinscale, CA12 5RH. OS ref: NY 25066 23596.
Loughrigg Tarn, LA22 9HF. OS ref: NY 34400 04300.

N

No Blade of Grass Cornel Wilde, 1970

'Yesterday, they were decent people letting their environment die. Now they are savages, killing to keep themselves alive...'

Certificate: PG
Producer: Cornel Wilde
Screenplay: Sean Forestal, Cornel Wilde, John Christopher (novel)
Music: Burnell Whibley
Colour: 88 minutes
Photography: H. A. R. Thomson
Cast: Nigel Davenport, Jean Wallace

The film is a classic case of man's inhumanity to man. 'Gone is the hope that life will go on' sings a sorrowful Roger Whittaker in the opening song on the soundtrack, setting the tone for all that follows. A poor polluted earth can take no more in American director Cornel Wilde's adaptation of John Christopher's haunting eco-apocalyptic 1956 sci-fi novel, *The Death of Grass*. Christopher (real name Sam Youd) also used a number of other pseudonyms for his mainstream literary career, which ran in parallel to a number of short stories that he wrote mainly for American science fiction magazines under the pen name John Christopher, though it was the success of his global catastrophe story that finally allowed him to concentrate solely on writing. In an introduction for a Modern classics reissue of the novel, acclaimed literary travel writer Robert Macfarlane added that the film was allegedly rechristened *No Blade of Grass* as the original title sounded too much like something out of a gardening catalogue.

If Christopher's original story was well received, Wilde's film version wasn't. This was despite using similar visual and narrative techniques to those he showed off in the African jungle drama *The Naked Prey* (1966) or brutal Japanese wartime movie *Beach Red* (1967). His bleak, pontifical re-working of Christopher's biological warfare story simply failed to resonate with audiences. The film makes no bones about its underlying ecological message, which is heavy handed and hammered home relentlessly throughout. A three minute opening montage features scrapped cars piled-up on top of each other, chimney stacks billowing plumes of thick orangey red smoke, whilst rivers emit lashings of polluted scum and exhausts splutter throughout capital cities gridlocked with traffic. It is all rather depressing.

Mankind is at fault for a highly contagious new virus (nicknamed 'Chung-

Li' after it emerges from the Far East) wiping out key members of the grass family. As a result, fundamental crops like rice and wheat are no longer available, bringing savage food and resource shortages worldwide. It isn't long before this spells doom for everyone. Sure enough, anarchy breaks out as starvation begins to hit home.

The late Nigel Davenport (*Chariots of Fire*) plays John Custance a London architect attempting to flee the city put under martial law with his family and close friend Roger (John Hamill – *Travels with my Aunt*), who works for the beleaguered Government. They head for the promise of peace and a plentiful supply of provisions at 'Blind Gill' a farm owned by John's brother in the Lake District, or Westmorland, as it is frequently called in the film (the county of Cumbria didn't arrive until four years after the film's release in 1974).

Davenport's trademark deep voice headed up a mainly English cast, that also included American actress Jean Wallace (who had married Wilde back in 1951) as Ann Custance, John's Canadian wife. Beautiful English rose, Lynne Frederick made her screen debut as their innocent teenage daughter Mary. Frederick famously went on to marry legendary actor Peter Sellers in her early twenties despite an age gap of some 30 years between them. She inherited almost his entire estate when he died of a heart attack, barely three years on, prompting many to label her a gold digger. An assertion clearly not helped when just six months later in 1981, she married small screen legend David Frost (pre-Knighthood), only to divorce him after they had spent just one year together.

Tragically, she went on to die from substance abuse aged only 39 in 1994. Even her first film role courted controversy with a rape scene that was cut from the UK release. It occurs shortly after John and the family head north, when Mary and her mother are ambushed by a group of bikers in a more lascivious than savage sequence. Especially when compared to other dystopian visions in films like *Mad Max* and *Dawn of the Dead* or the roaming gangs of Cormac McCarthy's novel *The Road*. The notorious scene was filmed at Park South level-crossing, near Barrow-in-Furness, a distinguished signal box still in use on the Cumbrian Coast Line, which runs from Carlisle to Barrow-in-Furness, before continuing to Carnforth, where it connects with the West Coast Main Line.

Its frame contains re-used pieces from a previous one at Coniston, demolished when its branch line closed in 1963. The film's cast also features former Eastenders actress Wendy Richard, who has a small cameo role as Clara, the sleazy girlfriend of untrustworthy Pirrie (Anthony May) who both end up joining the Custance exodus on the way out of London. After being forced to hand over their cars and possessions to an aggressive bunch of farmers, they meet a number of other roaming vagabonds under the distinctive frame of the Ribblehead Viaduct, on the Settle-Carlisle railway, which also features in

Park South signal box today.

the films; *Miss Potter* and *The Darkest Light*.

 The romantic shell of High Head Castle, near Ivegill, just a few miles south of Carlisle, is where the group seek temporary shelter, whilst a couple suffer the loss of their new-born baby during a painful birth scene. In 1956 a major fire destroyed much of High Head Castle, a Grade II listed building, leaving large parts of the property open and vulnerable to the elements. Originally built as a Pele Tower in the thirteenth century, it was extended and rebuilt for the Brougham family between 1744-9 in local red sandstone. English Heritage have already provided funding for a conservation management plan and undertaken emergency repairs to many parts of the structure. Together with the current owner, they are working to supply a long-term sustainable future for the property.

 Writing Youd's 2012 obituary in *The Guardian* newspaper, journalist Christopher Priest said the author made no effort to see the film until one day when it was shown on British television. Youd recalled settling down with a glass of whisky to watch it, but was safely tucked-up in bed by the end of the first commercial break.

Park South level crossing, LA16 7ER. Grid ref: SD 22077 77517.
High Head Castle, Ivegill, CA4 0PN. Grid ref: NY 40211 43502.

An A to Z: Cumbria and the Lake District on Film

Noble   Stephen Bradley, 2014

'A Fearless Life, A Reckless Love'

Certificate: PG-13   Colour: 100 minutes
Producers: Stephen Bradley, Melanie Gore-Grimes, Michael J. Hunt (executive), Nick Laws (line), Ngoc Luu (line)
Screenplay: Stephen Bradley   Photography: Trevor Forrest
Music: Ben Foster, Giles Martin
Cast: Deidre O'Kane, Sarah Greene, Brendan Coyle, Liam Cunningham, Ruth Negga, Gloria Cramer Curtis

Noble is a moving biopic about an Irish woman Christina Noble, who had a dream, which saved the lives of some 700,000 children. Her story is undoubtedly an inspiration and a classic case of triumph over considerable adversity. Born in Dublin 1944, her mother died when she was only ten-years-old. With her father unable to support the rest of the family, she subsequently endured a tortuous upbringing at the hands of a strict order of Nuns, who falsely declared her siblings were dead.

Eventually she escaped and lived homeless in Dublin where she was gang raped. She had a baby son who was adopted against her wishes before moving to the UK and settling in Birmingham. Eventually she had three more children after marrying a Greek Cypriot businessman, but the marriage turned sour as she fell victim to domestic abuse.

This part of her life unfolds against the background of the USA's disastrous war in Vietnam, and Christina has her fateful dream in the midst of all this personal anguish. She sees the word 'Vietnam' lit up in a bright light, with children appearing to reach out for help. After the traumatic events of her own childhood she believes it is the calling to a spiritual mission. Stephen Bradley (*Boy Eats Girl, Sweety Barrett*) wrote, directed and produced the screen adaptation of her life, which featured a predominantly Irish cast including his wife, Deidre O'Kane (*Intermission*) who played Christina in later life. The idea for the film actually came from O'Kane, after she hosted events for Christina's children's foundation during her time as a stand up comedian.

The script was mainly inspired by Christina's life story in her own unflinching book, *Bridge Across My Sorrow*, although Bradley stated he wanted to keep the film's story centred on hope rather than despair. Most of the film's significant moments are shown through a series of flashbacks. Yet it is always O'Kane's passages which anchor the story throughout, as she lands in Vietnam and metamorphoses into a humanitarian aid worker. Helping thousands of Vietnamese and Mongolian street children through a charitable foundation she has to fight hard to establish.

Apparently O'Kane shadowed Christina at her Vietnamese foundation for a couple of weeks prior to the start of filming. Touchingly, the real Christina

Present day tenement block in Barrow-in-Furness stands in for Dublin in the 1950s.

Noble appears at the end with some of the Vietnamese children who either feature in the film or are being supported by her Foundation.

Cork actress Sarah Greene (*Burnt, The Guard*) gives an impressive performance during the particularly harrowing events of her early adult-life and violent marriage. Brendan Coyle (probably best known as Lord Grantham's valet Mr Bates in ITV's award winning drama *Downton Abbey*) is Gerry Shaw, a wealthy Irish businessman stationed in Saigon who eventually helps Christina realise her vision. Debutant Gloria Cramer Curtis plays Christina during her poverty stricken childhood, when she begins an infatuation with American actress Doris Day whilst inhabiting the claustrophobic tenements of 1950s Dublin. Some of these scenes were filmed in the busy Victorian town of Barrow-in-Furness, (Cumbria's second largest urban area after Carlisle) which stands-in for Dublin. Lying at the tip of the Furness Peninsula opposite Morecambe Bay, facing the Duddon Estuary and Irish Sea, it boasts a proud industrial heritage, that developed into one of Britain's premier shipbuilding towns in the late nineteenth century.

Nowadays, visitors can investigate further at Barrow's fascinating Dock Museum, which has grown into one of the Lake District's most visited attractions boasting a number of free exhibits concentrating on the history of its associations with shipbuilding and steel production. As the town prospered and expanded a number of tenement blocks were erected in the 'Glasgow style' to help ease the immediate need for workers' housing. Built in the main by the architects Austin and Paley and Lancaster, they were constructed by an experienced Scottish builder. The Grade II listed Devonshire Buildings (named after the first Dock to open in 1867) are two impressive sandstone apartment buildings on Barrow Island owned by the Holker Estate. Situated on the main thoroughfare to the waterfront, they are still conveniently placed for the present day BAE Systems shipyard. Which retains a large workforce due to the Government's plans for the renewal of the UK's Trident nuclear deterrent.

The film took five years to come to fruition, including two for research, two for script writing/financing and then a year to shoot. Filming began in Vietnam throughout January 2013 in Ho Chi Minh City, at Saigon's District 5 where half of the film was shot. The cast and crew were greeted by the UK's wintry conditions in February, encountering snowfall at the tenements in Barrow, before moving on for a few days in Southport and Liverpool. Post-production took place in London before it premiered at the Santa Barbara International Film Festival, USA, in January 2014. Here it won the Panavision Award for Independent Cinema, the first of four festival awards in the same year. Bradley's film is certainly another fitting tribute to Christina's remarkable story. A life that back in 2003 was recognised for 'a lifetime of incredible achievement' and conferred with an Order of the British Empire by HRH Prince Charles.

Barrow-in-Furness, LA14 2SH. Grid ref: SD 19673 68209.

O

The One that Got Away

Roy Ward Baker (as Roy Baker), 1957

'He was daring, defiant and determined to escape'

Certificate: U Black and White: 111 minutes
Producers: David Deutsch (associate), Earl St. John (executive) and Julian Wintle
Photography: Eric Cross
Screenplay: Howard Clewes, Kendal Burt and James Leasor (book)
Music: Hubert Clifford
Cast: Hardy Krüger, Colin Gordon, Michael Goodliffe

Shortly after the film of German Luftwaffe pilot Oberleutnant Franz von Werra's story was released in December 1957, the grand old mansion Grizedale Hall (which features extensively in the Second World War film drama) was sadly all but knocked down. Situated near to the hamlets of Satterthwaite and Hawkshead, the building was surrounded by over 400 acres of woodland, and boasted some forty rooms. A wealthy merchant and shipowner named Harold Brocklebank from Irton had bought the Grizedale estate in 1903, before he set about completely rebuilding the Old Hall.

It was sold to the Forestry Commission in 1936, but was soon requisitioned by the Government in 1939 for use as a prisoner-of-war camp. It returned immediately afterwards to the Forestry Commission, eventually falling into disrepair from neglect. During its time as a POW camp, it became known as 'Special Camp No. 1' or more commonly by its nickname the 'U-boat Hotel' (due to the large amount of German U-Boat officers sent there).

Nowadays, the old Grizedale Hall is mainly associated with von Werra, who had been shot down at the height of the Battle of Britain over Kent on 5 September 1940 and transferred up to Cumbria after interrogation. Just a month later, on 7 October, he managed to escape from a working party outside the POW camp and survived on the open fells for six days in typically inhospitable Lake District weather conditions. After re-capture and another bodged escape attempt from a camp at Swanick, Derbyshire, he was finally sent to Canada, where he made a daring escape from a train bound for Montreal. Crossing the frozen-over St. Lawrence River to reach the USA (a neutral country at that stage); he then made the long journey back to Germany via Mexico and Panama.

It wasn't long before he met his final end though, when the Messerschmitt (Me109) fighter plane he was piloting came down in unknown circumstances off the Dutch coast on 25 October 1941. The film starred Hardy Krüger (*A Bridge Too Far*) as the flamboyant von Werra. Its screenplay had been adapted from a 1956 book by Kendal Burt and James Leason, which relayed the exploits of the only German prisoner of war to escape from Allied custody.

The remains of old Grizedale Hall and modern visitor centre (right).

A former member of the Hitler youth himself; at just sixteen, Krüger had been conscripted into the German infantry in 1944, where he was eventually captured by American forces after heavy fighting at the end of the war. With archetypal blonde hair and blue eyes, considered a definitive sign of Aryan origin, it was hardly surprising he went on to play numerous German soldiers when his acting career finally took off. The locations used during von Werra's escape from Grizedale Hall included Bowkerstead Farm Bridge over Grizedale Beck, where several scenes were filmed. A group of around 25 prisoners of war march out of the camp for their daily spot of exercise, stopping at the bridge to have a smoke. The quick thinking von Werra seizes the moment to drop down behind a stone wall, before running off into woodland.

Another couple of scenes were filmed at nearby Hob Gill, a striking waterfall (once the site of a bloomery used to make iron). The escapee jumps across a stream above the waterfall, close-by to a modern-day sculpture installed in a plunge pool. The artwork is part of a series of projects commissioned by the Forestry Commission to re-imagine Grizedale Forest as an international centre for art in the environment. It isn't limited to just sculpture though, as there have been live literature events, a number of outdoor film screenings from the Eden Arts 'Picnic Cinema' programme, along with the ever-popular mountain bike trails and Go-Ape tree top adventures.

Once a year in late November, Low Bowkerstead (just south of Satterthwaite) is also used as a car park for the Coppermines Grizedale Stages car rally. The scene where von Werra edges alongside a dry stone wall, before he is spotted by a couple of land army girls was filmed by a field gate there. The small village of Satterthwaite features when the detainees exercise along the valley road, past the impressive All Saints Church.

All Saints Church, Satterthwaite.

The history of the early chapel is unknown, before it was either re-built or restored around 1675. Back in 1914, the church was remodelled again with funds supplied by the Brocklebanks of Grizedale Hall, whose name adorns the interior in several places.

Grizedale, LA22 0QH. Grid ref: SD 33571 94386.
Satterthwaite, LA22 0QN. Grid ref: SD 33734 92873.

P

Pandaemonium   Julien Temple, 2000

*'Their poems have crossed centuries,
but now their secrets will be revealed'*

Certificate: PG-13   Colour: 124 minutes
Producers: Michael Kustow (co), Nick O'Hagan, Mike Phillips (executive), Jane Robertson (line), Tracey Scoffield (executive), David M. Thompson (executive).
Photography: John Lynch   Screenplay: Frank Cottrell Boyce
Music: Dario Marianelli
Cast: Linus Roache, John Hannah, Samantha Morton, Emily Woof

Julien Temple and Frank Cottrell Boyce's compelling story of the creative relationship between the Romantic poets Wordsworth and Coleridge is often exquisite to watch, but deeply biographically flawed. Temple openly admitted the latter in various interviews at the time, declaring he wanted the film to be an emotional response rather than one based on fact. Growing up in Somerset, he had often wandered the Quantock hills with his father, frequently treading in Coleridge's footsteps. It didn't take long before he developed an obsession with the poet's work.

Today visitors can walk from the Quantocks into Exmoor National Park along 'The Coleridge Way', a 36-mile breathtaking adventure from Nether Stowey to Porlock. With his Somerset upbringing, there really shouldn't have been any surprise that Temple chose to show the relationship of the two poets from Coleridge's point of view, depicting Wordsworth mostly as an uptight, prudish traitor, who sells out his revolutionary ideals before betraying his friendship with Coleridge. However, the film's main theme attempts to highlight how creativity and addiction continue to be relevant in our twenty-first century lives. Despite being overly sympathetic to Coleridge, Temple also portrays the poet as a rather sad figure, who ultimately becomes the first public junkie.

At the end of the film, Wordsworth's sister, Dorothy suffers a comparable fate as she degenerates into a screaming madwoman, similarly addicted to laudanum. Temple, who initially gained notoriety as director of the Sex Pistols mockumentary *The Great Rock & Roll Swindle* (1980) and the ill-received musical *Absolute Beginners* (1983) cast Linus Roache (*Batman*

Bowderbeck Cottage, Buttermere.

Begins) as a spiky haired Samuel Taylor Coleridge, who starts off as a charismatic revolutionary more akin to Johnny Rotten, before the milk of paradise turns him into a shipwrecked Jim Morrison.

In a deliberate move against type, Scottish actor John Hannah (*Four Weddings and A Funeral*) played William Wordsworth, whilst Emily Woof (*The Full Monty*) played the spirited Dorothy. Incredibly, Temple claimed he had no idea of Woof's intimate connections with Wordsworth. At the time of filming her late father Robert lived directly opposite the poet's celebrated home at Town End, during his tenure as chairman of the Wordsworth Trust! Twice Oscar nominated Samantha Morton (*Control*) completed the film's main quartet, as Sara Coleridge, the poet's long suffering wife. Other cast members included; Andy Serkis as the radical John Thelwall, before he went on to land the coveted role of Gollum in Peter Jackson's epic *Lord of the Rings* trilogy. Samuel West (*Notting Hill*) is the other so-called Lake poet, Robert Southey.

Filmed principally in Somerset, the main locations included the Quantock hills near the western side of Exmoor, an area that contained many childhood memories for the director. Shot overall in around eight weeks, they also filmed on location in London and spent a week in the Lake District. BBC films added some financial assistance to Temple's personal vision, but a relatively low budget with numerous locations meant the production team encountered its fair share of problems. These included finding a suitable cottage from the period to double as the Wordsworth's home in the Lakes. With Dove Cottage at Town End, Grasmere out of the running, they eventually settled upon the pretty and modest Bowderbeck cottage, overlooking the beautiful Buttermere valley.

William and Dorothy arrive there in the film on a horse-drawn carriage from the direction of Hassness point along the lake's eastern shore, accompanied by a narrated extract from Wordsworth's meditative poem 'Tintern Abbey'. After the Coleridge family join them in Cumberland; Sam, William

Upper and middle sections of Moss Force waterfall.

and Mary Hutchinson (Emma Fielding) his soon-to-be wife, take a stroll out to the dramatic Moss Force waterfall. It is situated just off Robinson on Moss Beck above the Newlands Pass, which connects the Newlands valley to Buttermere. The impressive force is formed of three sections with the upper part split in two by a large boulder perched high above the cascading waters flowing down the ravine below. Coleridge visited the waterfall in full fury himself in 1802, famously writing about it in a letter to Mary's sister, Sara Hutchinson, describing the upper cascade as 'an infinity of pearls and glass bulbs'. Today, the falls are a popular spot for both motorists and tour buses stopping at Newlands Hause, where two paths lead to the foot of the upper and middle sections.

Typically, most of the scenes filmed in the Lake District are rain-soaked, which had been exactly the kind of weather Temple wanted. In order to contrast the overcast and rugged landscape of Cumbria, against the brighter, softer Somerset locations.

Temple confesses during a revealing director's commentary as part of the extra features on the film's DVD release, 'You either like it or hate it. The film was meant to wind-up and annoy a lot of crusty, old professors.' He couldn't even resist a final twist in the end credits either, with a tacked-on sequence which sees Coleridge inhabit a modern-day London, visiting familiar landmarks such as the London Eye, Piccadilly Circus and Millennium Dome, accompanied by a booming kitsch dance-version of 'Xanadu'.

Hassness Point and Moss Force, Newlands Hause, Buttermere, CA13 9XA:
Grid ref: NY 17865 16688.

The Paradine Case

Alfred Hitchcock, 1947

'Nice people don't go murdering other people!'

Certificate: U Black and White: 125 minutes
Producer: David O. Selznick
Screenplay: David O. Selznick, Robert Hichens (novel)
Photography: Lee Garmes Music: Franz Waxman
Cast: Gregory Peck, Ann Todd, Charles Laughton, Alida Valli

Alfred Hitchcock came to film scenes for *The Paradine Case* in Cumbria just after the end of the Second World War. Unfortunately, the movie didn't turn out to be one of his personal favourites from the way he consistently dismissed it in later interviews. Plus, it marked the end of his relationship with the Hollywood studio of the illustrious, David O. Selznick (best known for producing *Gone with the Wind* and *The Third Man)*; becoming the last film he ever made for the Vanguard film production company.

He reportedly had a number of issues with Selznick's constant interference throughout the making of the film version, based on Robert Hichens' 1933 novel of the same name. Unfortunately, it had become something of a pet project to Selznick, who'd been waiting to shoot it ever since he'd bought the film rights. As a result, he insisted upon constant re-shoots and re-writes, alongside orchestrating cuts in the final editing, even overseeing the supervision of the film's musical score after Hitchcock's stalwart Bernard Herrmann had turned it down. Eventually, he appointed Franz Waxman, who would ironically go on to compose the *Rear Window* soundtrack. Yet, as if all that wasn't enough for Hitchcock to deal with, he also didn't approve of the actors cast in the lead roles, for his preferred choices: Laurence Olivier, Greta Garbo and Robert Newton were eventually replaced by the trio: Gregory Peck, Alida Valli and Louis Jourdan – Olivier was too busy preparing his version of *Hamlet,* whilst Garbo turned it down after a screen test, before promptly retiring from acting altogether!

Finally, there were the overblown production costs, exacerbated by a dramatic court scene in the film's climax that involved constructing an exact replica of a courtroom from London's imperious Old Bailey. Amazingly, a full mock-up was put together in just under three months, although it ballooned the film's outlays by an additional $70-80,000. In the end, its overall budget rocketed way out of control, mainly due to Selznick's tampering, with final cost estimations reputed at around $4 million, almost as much as *Gone With The Wind* – the most expensively produced film at that time.

The film's story is centred on Anna Paradine (Valli) who is placed on trial for the murder of her wealthy blind husband, a late middle-aged Colonel in the British Army. Anthony Keane (Peck) is hired to take on the case and quickly becomes infatuated by Anna's exotic beauty, despite being happily married. Keane travels to the Lake District to investigate the murder scene and visits the Paradine family estate, Hindley Hall against his client's wishes. Here he finds a disturbing looking portrait of Anna in her grandiose bedroom quarters inside the grand, mock Elizabethan manor house, really the Langdale Chase Hotel, originally built in 1891. Situated on the A591 near Low Wood on the eastern shore of Lake Windermere, close to Ambleside, this opulent country house also features in *The Dambusters*. While there, he runs into Anna's bit on the side, the unkempt dead man's valet, Andre Latour (Louis Jourdan) whom he hopes to pin the murder on.

Hitchcock introduces Keane to the Lake District via the old railway station at Braithwaite. Now long gone, the building survives only as a private house, yet traces of its former distinctive architectural features remain, including the rectilinear entrance where Hitchcock makes his trademark walk-on part behind Keane, as they both exit the station. Back when the film was made in 1947, there had been a railway line between Cockermouth and Penrith via Keswick, with Braithwaite one of the erstwhile stations en route.

Keane stays in bedroom number 17 at the Station Hotel – really the Drunken Duck Inn and Restaurant at Barngates, snuggled in the central Lake District, within touching distance of Tarn Hows, Ambleside and Hawkshead. The inn's name dates back unofficially to Victorian times, where according to local legend; a brace of tipsy ducks nearly ended up being roasted alive by a presumptuous landlady who'd found them strewn across the road. A small amount of beer had inadvertently drained into their feed, causing them all to nod off on the tarmac. Luckily for them, they awoke just in the nick of time, as a remorseful landlady knitted them all woollen waistcoats until their plucked feathers grew back!

Keane's journey the following morning from the Station Hotel to Hindley Hall is memorable for two other film locations he drives by along the way. Setting out in a horse-drawn two-seater carriage, he turns left out of the driveway to Yew Tree Farmhouse, Coniston, (which doubled as Beatrix Potter's Lakeland property 'Hill Top' 60 years later in *Miss Potter*). A little further on he passes the former St. John's Church (demolished in 1963) that used to stand tall in the serene village of Uldale, located in the northern Lake District, roughly ten miles from Keswick. He completes the journey riding over Middle Fell Bridge, Great Langdale (Laura and Alec's favourite place to linger in *Brief Encounter*).

The Drunken Duck Inn at Barngates, near Ambleside

AN A TO Z: CUMBRIA AND THE LAKE DISTRICT ON FILM

Let's face it, most Hollywood film productions stretch our common notions of reality, but a journey from the Drunken Duck Inn to the Langdale Chase Hotel via Uldale and Great Langdale is certainly taking the scenic route!

Langdale Chase Hotel, Windermere, LA23 1LW. Grid ref: NY 38676 01678.
Drunken Duck Inn, Barngates, LA22 0NG. Grid ref: NY 35061 01276.
Yew Tree Farm, Coniston, LA21 8DP. Grid ref: SD 31939 99839.
Uldale, CA7 1HA. Grid ref: NY 24983 36974.
Middle Fell Bridge, Langdale, LA22 9JU. Grid ref: SD 49723 70678.

❦ ❦ ❦ ❦ ❦

The Pike 1982, unmade

'A cold relentless killer from the murky depths'

Screenplay: Cliff Twemlow (novel)
Cast: Joan Collins, Jack Hedley, Linda Lou Allen

Imagine... *Jaws* on Windermere! Well, Cliff Twemlow dubbed 'The Orson Welles of Salford' did exactly that when he published *The Pike* in 1982. He quickly turned the book into a screenplay featuring a twelve foot long pike in a terrifying monster movie, to be set almost exclusively on England's largest lake. Twemlow even supplied a soundtrack, owned the production company and was due to play one of the leads! Although the undoubted starring role in the film would belong to a mechanical pike, controlled by computer and built by the Cumbrian firm Ulvatech, at a cost of $250,000.

Legendary actress Joan Collins had been signed up to play an unnamed woman helping reporters solve the mystery of the terrifying menace. During a special *Tomorrow's World* BBC TV report on the making of the film, she witnesses the

The 'enormous' model for the Pike at Low Wood, Windermere

109

huge model fish for the first time, describing it as 'enormous', although with no apparent idea of its actual size. Fresh from his role as Sir Timothy Havelock in the Bond film, *For Your Eyes Only* (1981) a suave looking Jack Hedley reveals he is down to play a marine biologist brought in to provide answers to the investigation. American actress Linda Lou Allen also features in the TV footage, although she is unaware of her intended role at the time.

Ultimately, the plug was pulled from the project due to the panning it received from the nation's press at a special promotion day. However, despite looking slightly battered, the large model fish still survives as a testament to Twemlow's imagination at the Low Wood Sports Centre upon Windermere. Where it lies in wait, hoping to be plunged into the murky depths once more.

The Plague Dogs   Martin Rosen, 1982

'Escape to a different World... And share the adventure of a lifetime'

Certificate: PG-13
Producer: Martin Rosen
Screenplay: Martin Rosen, Richard Adams (novel)
Cast: John Hurt, Christopher Benjamin, James Bolam

Colour: 103 minutes

Music: Patrick Gleeson

American born film-maker Michael Rosen wrote, produced and directed this rather bleak story based on a Richard Adams novel. In doing so, the film became the first animated feature to fully incorporate the Lake District landscape. Appropriately, Adams' 1977 novel also featured location maps drawn by renowned author and Cumbrian fell-walker Alfred Wainwright.

Released as a follow-up to the widely acclaimed animated adventure *Watership Down* (1978), the film is a fervent condemnation of the use of animals for experimental research. It includes the voices of legendary British actor John Hurt as Snitter – a fox terrier, and Christopher Benjamin as Rowf – a mixed Labrador-Retriever. Hurt had also voiced Hazel, the lead character in *Watership Down*, along with Nigel Hawthorne (*The Madness of King George*) as Capt. Campion. Hawthorne similarly returned in *The Plague Dogs* to voice the cagey Dr. Boycott, one of the inhumane 'white coats' who desperately try to keep a lid on Snitter and Rowf's escape from the Coniston research laboratory. Former *Likely Lad* actor James Bolam used a distinctive Cumbrian dialect voicing The Tod, a cunning fox who Snitter and Rowf regularly encounter on the open fells.

The various Lakeland locations drawn range from a relatively deserted Coniston village, where the two dogs go scrounging for food in the Co-op, a stone circle clearly reminiscent of Castlerigg near Keswick, some dis-used mine workings in Dunnerdale and the affectionately named, La'al Ratty, one of the oldest and longest narrow gauge railways in England. The army are called in to shoot the canine pair after word gets out that they have been infected by bubonic plague at the laboratory.

Who let the dogs out? Rowf, The Tod and Snitter on the run.
© Photos 12/Alamy Stock Photo.

Snitter and Rowf try to escape the enclosing forces by sneaking aboard a train at Dalegarth station in Eskdale before arriving at Ravenglass, the only coastal town in the National Park. Unfortunately, they have nowhere left to run as they head towards the empty sea before swimming out to the sanctuary of a seemingly mythical island.

Oddly, the film was produced by Nepenthe Productions; 'Nepenthe' a drug or a drink, had originally been described in Homer's *Odyssey* as having the power to banish grief or trouble from a person's mind. Yet the film does the exact opposite, as it focuses mainly on the cruelty of mankind with a distressing and gloomy storyline. One of its distributors Embassy Pictures were so worried that they ordered significant cuts to be made for US audiences. As a result, a number of different versions became available on subsequent DVD releases. Although a full 103-minute cut was finally released in the UK back in 2008.

AN A TO Z: CUMBRIA AND THE LAKE DISTRICT ON FILM
Postman Pat: The Movie

Mike Disa, 2014

'He's first class!'

Certificate: U Colour: 88 minutes
Producer: Robert Anich (as Robert Anich Cole)
Screenplay: Annika Bluhm, Nicole Dubuc, Kim Fuller
Music: Rupert Gregson-Williams
Cast: Jim Broadbent, Susan Duerden, Stephen Mangan, David Tennant

Since his debut over 30 years ago on BBC One in 1981, Postman Pat has gone on to become one of the world's most beloved children's characters. Originally he was brought to life by John Cunliffe, a former Kendal teacher who re-imagined the near-by valley of Longsleddale as the fictional village of Greendale, Pat's green and pleasant hometown. A single snakelike track winds its way delicately through the isolated valley, situated four miles to the north-west of Kendal. Most of the scattered cottages amongst the pastoral landscape were built as small farms dating from the seventeenth century; little has changed since. Once an important route for packhorse traffic coming down from Scotland to the south or the west, these days Longsleddale is a veritable haven for walkers who come to trek across to Staveley or Kentmere, or tackle the Gatesgarth Pass over to Haweswater and beyond.

A former sub post-office on Kendal's Beast Banks provided the main inspiration for Greendale's similar looking outlet, which is run by the endearing Mrs Goggins. A tea drinking Scottish postmistress who sorts all the letters and parcels before Pat takes them out on his daily rounds. The first television series was directed by the animator Ivor Wood, who also worked on a few other children's favourites such as: *The Magic Roundabout* and *Paddington Bear*. Yet for many kids it is Pat, along with Jess (his faithful ol' black and white cat) who has always been the complete package. After numerous television spin-offs, work finally began on a debut big screen 3D animated adventure shortly after Pat celebrated his thirtieth birthday. Directed by a former animator at Disney, American Mike Disa, it was produced by Lionsgate Films, (who gained huge success with 2012's dystopian fantasy *The Hunger Games*) and Icon Productions which had been set up by the Australian actor/director Mel Gibson in 1989.

The film version boasts a strong cast of British Hollywood A-Listers, including: Stephen Mangan as the voice of Pat, Oscar winner Jim Broadbent, former *Doctor Who* David Tennant and Rupert Grint, fresh from playing the maddening Ron Weasley in the hugely successful *Harry Potter* series of films. It sets out to show how delivering post isn't Pat's only forté, with

Pat and Jess encounter farmer Alf Thompson looking a bit sheepish
© 2014 RGH Pictures and Classic Media. All rights reserved.

Boyzone singer Ronan Keating supplying his singing voice during an audition for the television talent show, *You're the One* which arrives with a big fanfare in Greendale.

Desperate to finance a proper honeymoon to Italy for his wife Sara (Susan Duerden) Pat instantly woos the subtly named Simon Cowbell (Robin Atkin Downes) with a captivating singing voice, forcing the talent-spotter to proclaim, 'You know how to deliver!' However, things take a rather sinister turn when Pat is whisked away to the bright lights of London seeking fame and fortune, leaving behind a vacancy in the Greendale delivery office. His dubious replacement arrives in the form of a 'PatBot 3000' a super-efficient robotic postman, replete with a dodgy toothy grin and scary eyes that glow red! The most important things to the new Pat are: efficiency, profit and success. The callous android ushers in the film's contrasting theme of simple rural life set against the technology, money and power of the big city. Pat's new cyber creation also heralds the first stage of an outlandish attempt for world domination by a villainous corporate tablet-weaving upstart called Carbuncle (Peter Woodward).

In a 2011 interview for the *Westmorland Gazette* newspaper, Pat's creator (who now lives in Ilkley, West Yorkshire) stopped short of giving the film version his full stamp of approval. Bemoaning the Hollywood-isation of his once cheery character, he feared Pat would be changed out of all recognition. The resulting film's dark undertones and corporate satire are clearly proof that he was right to raise an eyebrow or two. These underlying themes helped keep adults in the audience attentive by parodying other more grown-up films, in particular the *Terminator-esque* Jess-Bot firing red lasers out of its eyes.

Fans of Kubrick's masterpiece *2001: A Space Odyssey* will undoubtedly recognise the moment when Pat-Bot breaks down and starts singing 'Daisy Daisy' a la Hal, after Wilf (David Tennant) holds a magnet to his face.

Thankfully, Cunliffe seemed in good spirits when interviewed after the film's sun-kissed Lake District premiere at the Brewery Arts Centre in Kendal, May 2014. A smile must have crossed his lips when contemplating the irony of how he dreamt up Pat just 100 yards away above the cinema complex in a small terraced cottage on Kendal's Greenside. Although he probably never envisaged his creation would ever body-pop along to a rendition of Stevie Wonder's 'Signed, Sealed, Delivered I'm Yours' the way he does during the film's final song and dance routine!

Longsleddale, LA8 9BB. Grid ref: NY 50132 02891.
Beast Banks, Kendal, LA9 5HG. Grid ref: SD 51282 91183.

R

Radiator Tom Browne, 2014
'How time changes parents into children and children into parents'

Certificate: 15 Colour: 93 minutes
Producers: Mel Agace (executive), Barbara Broccoli (executive), Tom Browne, Johnnie Frankel (executive), Jess Gormley (associate), Daniel Kleinman (executive), Ringan Ledwidge (executive), Mike Morrison (associate), Genevieve Stevens, Paul Harry Thomas (executive), Rachel Weisz (executive), Michael G. Wilson (executive).
Screenplay: Tom Browne, Daniel Cerqueira Photography: David Johnson
Music: Simon Allen
Cast: Daniel Cerqueira, Richard Johnson, Gemma Jones

Tom Browne's directorial debut has at its core the duel themes of caring for an ageing parent amidst comparative domestic chaos. Often moving and incredibly poignant, the film is an intimate family portrait featuring stunning performances rich with flashes of dark humour, despite a dismal, yet truthful subject matter. It was shot almost entirely in Browne's late parents' cottage in the small village of Mosedale, a home that had been left untouched since their deaths in 2011 and 2012. Over recent years care for the elderly has been referred to as society's 'elephant in the room' due to the UK's increasingly ageing population. For many living through an age of austerity, the extra financial strains of putting care in place for elderly parents can seem daunting. So perhaps there should be no real surprise that a film containing strands of these present day concerns, should arrive to shine a light on the kind of situations already facing numerous families.

In a career spanning almost twenty years, Browne is now firmly established as both an actor and film-maker. Back in 2000, he co-wrote and starred in the cult film *The Nine Lives of Tomas Katz*, whilst he has also acted (under the name Tom Fisher) for a host of distinguished director's such as: Jean-Marc Vallée in the period drama, *Young Victoria* (2009), Woody Allen in *Cassandra's Dream* (2007) and Stephen Sommers for the *The Mummy Returns* (2001). His first short film as a Director (*Spunkbubble*) premiered at the London Film Festival in 2009. That film also starred Daniel Cerqueira with whom he also co-wrote the screenplay for *Radiator*.

The idea to write specifically about Browne's parents came from Cerqueira, although penning the script took them three years, as they were not working to a specific time-frame. Despite the gradual developments, writing progressed organically, and once completed they were able to begin shooting relatively quickly. Somewhat bizarrely, the idea of asking Gemma Jones to play Browne's mother Maria had been hatched after they'd both worked over ten years before in Jackie Chan's action adventure *Shanghai Knights*. Intriguingly, Jones' first ever feature film role had been playing Oliver Reed's wife Madeleine in Ken Russell's highly controversial 1971 film *The Devils*. However, according to Jones, Russell let her off relatively lightly, as she didn't have to do anything too alarming! Curiously, her movie career only started to blossom some twenty years later after she played Mrs Dashwood in Ang Lee's 1995 lavish production of *Sense and Sensibility*. A couple of stints as Renée Zellweger's mum in the film adaptation of Helen Fielding's *Bridget Jones* novels followed. More recently, her fame spread to a younger audience after playing school nurse, Madam Poppy Pomfrey in three of the *Harry Potter* films.

Richard Johnson a RADA trained veteran of stage and screen (now aged in his late eighties) delivers a stand out performance as Leonard, Tom's eccentric and difficult father. In the prime of his youth, a devil may care attitude with good looks to match saw Johnson rise to fame in the late 1960s playing the British agent, 'Bulldog Drummond' in Ralph Thomas' screen adaptations of H. C. McNeile's fictional character. Cerqueira himself took on Tom's role, playing the often bemused middle-aged son Daniel, who Maria turns to for help with Leonard. Browne chose to shoot the film at his parents' old cottage in Mosedale mainly for practical reasons. Seeing as the overall budget came in at a paltry £145,000, the chance to use a visually striking and 'free' location could simply not be passed up.

Jones remarked that it felt like walking into someone's home when they arrived on set with all of Tom's parents' belongings still strewn haphazardly about the place. A cluttered, un-modernised home containing generations of history also mirrors the glacial landscape of Cumbria glimpsed in the scenes outside the confines of the house. The village of Mosedale lies on the River Caldew in the north-west corner of the Lake District, about eight miles from Keswick just off the A66. It is also a mile north of the small village of Mungrisdale, which is a popular starting point for walkers tackling the Northern Fells containing satellites from the impressive mountain, Blencathra. Bowscale Fell, Carrock Fell and Bannerdale Crags form a trio of mid-ranged hills close by.

According to Browne, the inhabitants of Mosedale were hugely supportive to the project, allowing the crew to use the eighteenth century Quaker Meeting House in the heart of the village, as a kitchen and dining room.

Obviously filming in an old cottage brought its fair share of challenges, but thanks to a superb crew they were able to suitably adapt to their cramped surroundings, using the outside lavatory and woodshed as storage places. One of the runners even found a local supplier for a constant stream of mice who are seen scurrying in and out of the furniture. In much the same way as the hungry pests who run riot in Beatrix Potter's *Tale of Samuel Whiskers*. A

Setting-up to film Daniel and Leonard on Derwentwater,
© 2014 Turnchapel Films.

bedroom also served as a greenroom, costume and make-up room, giving the actors a place of retreat to relax in relative warmth.

Other locations used included nearby places such as: Mosedale Moss, Bowscale Tarn and the summit of Carrock Fell, which Daniel escapes to after a particularly fraught episode with Leonard. Samuel Taylor Coleridge memorably described a stormy encounter atop Carrock Fell in a letter to his close friend the scientist Humphry Davy in 1800. The 'fearful' and 'tyrranous' winds he encountered there provoked genuine concerns that the summit cones might topple over as he sheltered beneath them. Wordsworth had already moved in at Dove Cottage when he passed by Mosedale with Coleridge on their Scottish walking tour of August 1803.

A few years afterwards, Bowscale Tarn situated beneath Tarn Crags on Bowscale Fell became known as the 'Tarn of the Immortal Fish' thanks to his considerable storytelling powers. He mentioned the local tradition of two immortal fish (sometimes referred to as 'Adam & Eve') swimming about in open sight during his 'Song at the Feast of Brougham Castle' (1807). Apparently one of them even had the ability to talk depending on which folk tale you read! The main subject of Wordsworth's poem was Henry Lord Clifford, a partisan of the House of Lancaster, who had been deprived of his estate after the decisive bloodbath at Towton Field in 1461. This gruesome battle proved to be a crushing defeat, which shattered the Lancastrians during the Wars of the Roses. Afterwards he lived for 24 years as a shepherd in Yorkshire and in the former county of Cumberland, where the estate of his father-in-law, Sir Lancelot Threlkeld was situated. Henry VII eventually restored his estate in the first year of his reign.

Adding a further layer of depth to several of the film's poetic moments is a score from Simon Allen who produced otherworldly sound pieces with an Aeolian harp. It had initially been Browne's idea to include music with a strong natural element to it. Named after Aeolus, the ancient Greek God of the wind, the harp's ethereal sounds became fashionable during the Romantic era and a reputed favourite of Wordsworth and Coleridge. Recalling his childhood, Daniel finally manages to get Leonard off the sofa to take him out in a rowing boat. In a scene filmed on Derwentwater they sail his old wooden toy boats, giving a vital element of space to the film.

Other location shots were filmed in Penrith when Daniel visits a solicitor's and a cafe. There are also juxtapositions with his life in the city, after he temporarily escapes back to London when Maria returns from a small break away at a friends' house. One of Browne's favourite moments in the film is the hugely symbolic shot of the fireplace with the fire gone out. Although a relatively simple image, it perfectly captures a sense of the end of life, another major theme. The film premiered at the London Film Festival in October 2014, before a triumphant 'homecoming' screening (attended by a number of locals from Mosedale) at the 16th Keswick Film Festival in February 2015.

Mosedale, CA11 0XQ. Grid ref: NY 35711 32210.
Carrock Fell, CA7 9JS. Grid ref: NY 34184 33620.
Derwentwater, CA12 5UB. Grid ref: NY 25992 21055.
Penrith, CA11 9DU. Grid ref: NY 50977 30013.

༺ ༺ ༺ ༺ ༺

The Raven on the Jetty

Erik Knudsen, 2014

'In the midst of separation, one boy's longing has the power to change everything'

Certificate: 15   Colour: 88 minutes
Producers: Erik Knudsen, Janet Knudsen   Screenplay: Erik Knudsen
Photography: Mark Duggan, Erik Knudsen
Cast: Anne Fraser, Anne Lees, Connor O'Hara, Rob O'Hara, Helen Teasdale

This is a contemplative film from the independent production and distribution company: One Day Films Limited. It was shot entirely on location in Lancashire and Cumbria, and directed by Erik Knudsen, Professor of Film Practice at the University of Salford in Manchester. Born to Ghanian and Danish parents, Knudsen gained a Phd at Salford in 2002 with a thesis entitled: *The Dispassionate Mirror – Towards a Transcendental Realism in Film Practice*. One of the paper's themes included 'understanding life through feeling', which is particularly evident in the reflective story about a young boy, Thomas (played by eleven-year-old Connor O'Hara), who finds himself in a lonely void as a result of the separation of his parents.

Selected for the 15th Keswick Film Festival and screened at the Theatre by the Lake in March 2014, it also won the Jury Award at the Madrid International Film Festival, Spain, before being selected for the inaugural Aberdeen Film Festival, in October of the same year. The film predominately featured a Cumbrian cast and crew with Connor's real life father Rob, from Ulverston playing Thomas's onscreen father. Helen Teasdale (originally from Leeds, but now settled in Carlisle) played his mother. The raven known as Cadge came from the Silverband Falconry in the Eden Valley, on the eastern edge of the Lake District, at Whiteacres, Kirkby Thore, near Penrith. One of the main themes Knudsen wanted to incorporate was the transition from a city to a rural lifestyle. This is shown over a two-day period when Thomas travels on his ninth birthday with his mother to the seafront at Morecambe Bay on the southern border of Cumbria, where they call on his maternal grandmother.

Cedric Robinson MBE was royally appointed as the Queen's guide to the sands that incorporate over 120 square miles (when the tide goes out). In May

*Thomas faces the Raven on the shores of Ullswater,
© One Day Films.*

2014, he received the Freedom of the City of Lancaster in recognition of 40 years assisting people with the safe crossing of Morecambe Bay. Often billed as a 'mini-Blackpool' the promenade is still home to a number of family-run hotels, whilst the refurbished Midland Hotel opposite the railway station is a classic example of the ocean liner Art Deco style of the 1930s. Another highlight is the larger-than-life statue of comedian Eric Morecambe bringing sunshine to thousands of visitors since the Queen unveiled it in 1999. Just across the road from Eric is the Old Pier Bookshop, an undoubted Aladdin's cave for bookworms filled with pearls awaiting discovery.

In the film the spectacular view across the bay to the Lakeland Mountains indicates the direction where Thomas and his mother are heading next. The following morning they set off north by car to visit his estranged father at a very remote farmhouse in the Lake District. These scenes were filmed near Reagill, a delightful village in the unspoilt Eden Valley close to Penrith. The 17th century building in the middle of nowhere plays a central role in the film. Knudsen portrays it as a potent symbol of Thomas's father, who has abandoned urban living in favour of an isolated rural life. As a child of the digital age, Thomas's encounter with the natural world, and his gradual understanding of the pivotal connection he provides for his ultimately lonely parents, leads to a journey of self-realisation and discovery.

Scenes where Thomas confronts the raven were filmed at a private jetty on the west side of Ullswater, near Watermillock. Originally Knudsen had planned on shooting at a wooden jetty on Derwentwater, but was forced to change his plan due to problems gaining filming permissions and growing concerns over the location's popularity with visitors. A decision that ultimately worked in his favour, when he later acknowledged the stone jetty and boat house contained exactly the type of 'abandoned feel' that he had been searching for. Other locations included private woods near Kings Meaburn in the Eden valley (a place steeped in the history of a former Lord of the Manor – Hugh de Morville, who was implicated in the infamous murder of the Archbishop of Canterbury Saint Thomas A'Beckett in 1170).

Scenes were also filmed at a house in the west Cumbrian village of Seaton (on the north side of the River Derwent across from Workington) and the petrol station at Rheged, just off the A66 on the cusp of Penrith.

Morecambe Bay, LA23 2XH. Grid ref: SD 33238 62288.
Reagill, CA10 3ER. Grid ref: NY 60383 17504.
Ullswater, CA11 0JS. Grid ref: NY 42772 20387.
Kings Meaburn, CA10 3BU. Grid ref: NY 62099 21097.
Rheged Centre, CA11 0DQ. Grid ref: NY 49692 28316.

S

She'll be Wearing Pink Pyjamas

John Goldschmidt, 1985

'Life isn't a rehearsal you know, this is it!'

Certificate: 15 Colour: 86 minutes
Producers: Adrian Hughes (co), David McFarlane (associate), Tara Prem
Screenplay: Eva Hardy (novel) Photography: Clive Tickner
Music: John Du Prez
Cast: Julie Waters, Anthony Higgins

A film based on the real life experiences of screenwriter Eva Hardy; the story follows eight British women from varying backgrounds through a week long survival course at an outward-bound centre in the Lake District. Julie Walters stars as Fran, a rambling 30 something on a three-year abstention from sex. Unfortunately, the film flopped as a follow-up to the hugely successful *Educating Rita* released the previous year, where Walters received an Oscar nomination playing the lead role. However, *She'll Be Wearing Pink Pyjamas* did become known for one thing – a shower scene, where the actresses, cameramen and sound crew all ended up filming in the altogether!

Walters recalled how her fellow thespians played a trick on the sound crew one night in a pub, convincing them Equity had passed a new motion stating crews were required to get naked if the actors did. Somehow their cunning plan worked, as the crew foolishly believed them! It must have been quite an eyeful with everyone completely starkers during filming; apparently the sound man remained undeterred clutching a boom mic, and cameraman, Clive Tickner just sat there happily oblivious with nothing but headphones on!

Other members of the cast included a number of British TV and film actresses with Janet Henfrey as Lucy, Alyson Spiro as Tina, and Anthony Higgins as Tom. The magnificent landscape topography of Eskdale is steeped in history and provides a stunning backdrop to the locations used throughout the film. For a base the women stay at Gate House, a Grade II listed Outward Bound Centre on Smithybrow Lane. These days the site is set in 60 acres of landscaped grounds amidst glorious scenery taking in some of England's most spectacular and highest mountains, with a tarn and Japanese garden to relax in for good measure.

Just up the road from the unspoilt village of Eskdale Green, the centre now serves as a haven of peace and tranquillity for those wishing to escape the everyday pressures of modern life. Fran and her fellow companions stay in a bunk-styled dormitory, with shared facilities, as if trying to add a boot-camp mentality to proceedings. Another location used nearby to the Outward Bound Centre was Trough House Bridge, a picturesque packhorse bridge spanning the River Esk near to Stanley Ghyll, probably dating from the eighteenth century.

Trough House Bridge on the River Esk, Eskdale.

One by one, the women conquer their collective fears by jumping off the old bridge into the clear, bubbling waters of the Esk. In a later interview, Alyson Spiro (Tina) recalled how panicked she felt at the height of the bridge, though her jump worked out fine, thanks to the help of an underwater stunt co-ordinator who was waiting to fish her out. During another activity Fran capsizes repeatedly attempting to kayak underneath the Arnside viaduct on the Kent estuary. Eventually, the eight women split into two groups for the film's main event – a two-day hike up to Scafell Pike, England's highest mountain at 3,210ft. There is one memorable panoramic shot of a group together on top of Scafell, as the camera swings around the summit cairn from the westerly direction of Wastwater, looking up towards the well-known pyramid shape of Scafell Pike, beckoning in the distance. There are many trials and tribulations for all of the women along the way, before Walters triumphantly slides into the Gate House Centre on a zip wire, dressed in some very bright and baggy looking pyjamas.

Eskdale, CA19 1TX. Grid ref: NY 14148 00184.

⚜ ⚜ ⚜ ⚜ ⚜

Sightseers Ben Wheatley, 2012

'Evil has a knitted jumper!'

Certificate: 15 Colour: 88 minutes
Producers: James Biddle (co), Jenny Borgars (executive), Katherine Butler (executive), Tamzin Cary (associate), Claire Jones, Matthew Justice (executive), Nira Park, Danny Perkins (executive), Celia Richards (associate), Andrew Starke (as Andy Starke), Edgar Wright (executive).
Screenplay: Alice Lowe, Steve Oram   Photography: Laurie Rose
Music: Jim Williams
Cast: Alice Lowe, Steve Oram, Eileen Davies

It's not often you see locations such as a National Tramway and Pencil Museum in the same film, not to mention an ancient stone circle and Petrifying Well. But that's exactly what awaits in this dark, gruesome, black comedy about a couple of nerds from the Midlands who embark on an ill-fated road trip across the rural parts of northern England. Cumbrian locations feature extensively in a number of scenes, ranging from the mystical Long Meg and Her Daughters stone circle (near Penrith), to the slate-quarried Honister pass.

A visit to the museum marking the birthplace of the pencil nods to a history that began in Cumbria back in the early sixteenth century, long before the first tourists came to Lakeland. Legends say how one night a violent storm uprooted a number of trees at the head of the Borrowdale area. Despite the wind's savage destruction, a day or two later some of the locals found an unusual dark coloured material amongst the upturned roots, which turned out to be graphite. It didn't take long before shepherds were using the new black substance to mark sheep with, as a cottage industry sprung up, which eventually led to the opening of the UK's first pencil factory in 1832 at Keswick, then the so-called 'pencil capital of the world'. Almost 200 years later in 2011, the Cumberland Pencil Museum celebrated its 30th birthday, having transformed a former factory canteen into a highly successful visitor attraction, welcoming over 80,000 visitors a year.

Sightseers became British director Ben Wheatley's third outing, having previously made the equally unnerving *Down Terrace*, *Kill List* and highly rated *A Field in England*. It was co-written by the stand-up comedians, Alice Lowe (Tina) and Steve Oram (Chris – Tina's new boyfriend). Their dream caravan holiday quickly takes a seriously wrong turn when they end up embarking on a ruthless killing spree, akin to a modern day Bonnie & Clyde clad in anoraks. Chris refers to himself as a writer with 'creative constipation' who also suffers with an intolerance of: yobbish litterbugs, noisy teenagers, pre-booked caravan sites and stuck-up National Trust Members!

His beloved Abbey Oxford caravan initially takes Tina away from her sheltered lifestyle and meddling mother, as he sets out to show her the supposedly 'precious things' in his world. These 'things' include some of the most bizarre tourist attractions across Derbyshire, Yorkshire and Cumbria. Halfway through their macabre misadventures, Tina visits Keswick's fantastic Pencil Museum, purchasing a huge 'big scribbler' for £24 in the gift shop to write a note to Chris in the cafeteria. They stop-off at Long Meg and Her Daughters, the second largest stone circle in the UK near Little Salkeld on the outskirts of Penrith. An ancient site with 69 stones made out of local red sandstone and thought to date back to 1,500BC.

At the stone circle they encounter an outspoken National Trust member played by Richard Lumsden (*Downhill*) – Kenneth Branagh's ex-brother-in-law. Unfortunately he inadvertently reprimands Tina for letting her dog Poppy foul the grass around the site and threatens to inform the National Trust if she doesn't pick it up immediately. This is of course a big mistake, especially as Chris then cooks up a lewd scenario, which spells disaster for the pernickety rambler. His bloody end is strangely reminiscent of the moment in Stanley Kubrick's sci-fi epic, *2001: A Space Odyssey (1968)* when Moon-watcher infamously beats a fellow ape to a pulp. Afterwards, Tina reflects how she'd never thought about killing an innocent person before, to which Chris deadpans the films' most memorable line 'he's not a person Tina, he's a *Daily Mail* reader!'

Long Meg faces her stone circle, Little Salkeld.

Other Cumbrian locations Wheatley decided to use included the Park Cliffe camping and caravan campsite near Bowness on Windermere, where Chris meets his new best-mate Martin (Roger Glover – *A Field in England*). Later they arrange to hook-up again at a lay-by on the B5289 Honister Pass, near to the slate mine. At 1,200 feet, it is easily one of the highest passes in the Lake District. Here, Martin inevitably meets a sticky-end after he refuses Tina's drunken advances!

Tina and Chris leave behind a gruesome trail,
© Photos 12/Alamy Stock Photo.

Throughout the film there is a painful, uncomfortableness broken up only by Ben Wheatley's use of haunting cinematography, which eerily shows off the increasingly isolated landscapes Tina and Chris find themselves in. The overall brooding effect is like a cross between the menacing darkness of Royston Vasey's *League of Gentleman* and Mike Leigh's self-righteous campers during *Nuts in May*. However, new levels of creepiness were reached in August 2013, when the film was screened by the Eden Arts Picnic Cinema programme in the courtyard of Keswick's Pencil Museum!

Long Meg and Her Daughters, CA10 1NW. Grid ref: NY 57183 36940.
The Pencil Museum, Keswick, CA12 5NG. Grid ref: NY 26343 2380
Park Cliffe, Windermere, LA23 3PG. Grid ref: SD 39090 91124.
Honister Pass, CA12 5XJ. Grid ref: NY 23518 12151.

Snow White and the Huntsman
Rupert Sanders, 2012
'The Fairytale is over!'

Certificate: PG-13   Colour: 127 minutes
Producers: Laurie Boccaccio (associate), Gloria S. Borders (executive), Sarah Bradshaw (co), Helen Hayden, Sam Mercer, Palak Patel, Joe Roth.
Screenplay: Evan Daugherty, John Lee Hancock, Hossein Amini.
Photography: Greig Fraser   Music: James Newton Howard
Cast: Kristen Stewart, Chris Hemsworth, Charlize Theron.

Evil fights destiny in this epic fantasy adventure, with teen pin-up Kristen Stewart (*Twilight*) cast as Princess Snow White, the only person fairer than Queen Ravenna, played by a sultry Charlize Theron (*Monster*). According to the old fairy tale, the devilish Queen as we all know is out to kill her. However, in a twist to the traditional story, Ravenna promises to bring the dead wife of a Huntsman (Chris Hemsworth – *Thor*) back to life, but only if he can deliver Snow White to her after the Princess flees to the Dark Forest. Nevertheless, upon discovering the wicked ruler has lied to him, the Huntsman decides to protect the isolated Princess instead. Eventually they stumble across a band of dwarves, (played by a who's who of British actors, including: Ray Winstone, Bob Hoskins and Ian McShane amongst others) whilst roaming through a magic fairy land. The scene is then set for a final showdown with the evil Queen, who has learnt from her infamous Magic-Mirror that Snow White will destroy her unless she can consume her heart to become immortal.

Hollywood arrived in the Lake District during October 2011 when shooting on the fantasy blockbuster (based on the German fairytale *Little Snow White*) took place at Cathedral Cave, Little Langdale and close to the tourist honey-pot, Blea Tarn. Cathedral Cave is part of a minor network of interlinked slate quarries located near Ambleside. Owned by the National Trust, they are best known for an impressive main chamber, which never fails to have an impact on any unsuspecting walkers, standing at some forty feet in height and lit dramatically by two openings off the main site. There is a quick glimpse of Snow White, the Huntsman and band of dwarves moving swiftly through it in the film.

After the funeral of Gus, the remaining group march over a stream on the open fells in heavy, driving rain, just below the picturesque Blea Tarn at Great Langdale. Apparently because of the dreadful wet weather conditions during filming there was absolutely no need to add any CGI rain effects afterwards! However, the shoot slowed down as a result, but thankfully continued roughly on schedule due to the local National Trust farmers, who helped manoeuvre

Cathedral Cave, Little Langdale.

the film crew's equipment using quad bikes. The Cumbrian scenes represented the only time production moved away from Pinewood Studios, Buckinghamshire on the outskirts of London. Only the principal actors and stunt-doubles of the real dwarves (aptly nicknamed Mini-Me's) were used to film in the Lake District.

Originally published by the Brothers Grimm exactly 200 years before in 1812, the Universal Pictures makeover proved to be a big box office hit. It marked the directorial debut of Englishman Rupert Sanders, whose wife Liberty Ross also featured in the film as Snow White's mother, Queen Eleanor. The glamorous pairing of Oscar winning actress Theron with teen heartthrob Stewart, alongside the macho Australian actor Hemsworth, certainly guaranteed the lavish production a high profile.

The film also received a couple of Oscar nominations for Best Costume Design and Best Visual Effects. Unsurprisingly, both Sanders and Stewart dropped out of the 2016 sequel (*The Huntsman: Winter's War*). Their brief and ill-fated fling was sensationally exposed when the couple were well and truly caught out kissing on camera in July 2012. As a result, the celebrity gossip magazine, *US Weekly* published the devastating pictures, prompting Sanders' wife to file for divorce immediately. Whilst Stewart's actor boyfriend and *Twilight Saga* co-star Robert Pattinson chose to forgive her.

Three Shires Inn (for Cathedral Cave), LA22 9NZ. Grid ref: NY 31660 03400.

AN A TO Z: CUMBRIA AND THE LAKE DISTRICT ON FILM
Soft Top Hard Shoulder

Stefan Schwartz, 1993

'It's a terrific, good-time comedy'

Certificate: 15
Producer: Richard Holmes
Photography: Henry Braham
Colour: 89 minutes
Screenplay: Peter Capaldi
Music: Chris Rea
Cast: Peter Capaldi, Frances Barber, Catherine Russell, Jeremy Northam, Richard Wilson

The Glaswegian Time Lord – Peter Capaldi, wrote and starred in this low-budget road movie homage to director and fellow Scot, Bill Forsyth (*Gregory's Girl*). Previously best-known for his role as the foul-mouthed spin-doctor, Malcolm Tucker in the BBC's political satire *The Thick of It*, Capaldi's breakthrough came when he played the role of Danny Oldsen in Forsyth's major commercial hit *Local Hero*, released in 1983. Ironically, back in 1989, *Soft Top's* director Stefan Schwartz appeared in an acting role for three *Doctor Who* episodes, playing a Knight Commander opposite Sylvester McCoy, (then the seventh Doctor). Set in the village of Pennan, Aberdeenshire, Forsyth's *Local Hero* came top in a poll for the most atmospheric use of a British film location in 2005. It famously starred Hollywood legend Burt Lancaster (*Bird Man of Alcatraz*), who played Felix Happer, an oil magnate who sends a representative to the tiny village to investigate building a refinery.

The film's enduring legacy is still apparent some 30 years on, judging by the amount of tourists who continue journeying to Pennan, to have their photo taken next to Gilbert Scott's iconic red telephone box. In another tribute to Forsyth's film, Capaldi is pictured in front of a red phone box with co-star Elaine Collins (his wife in real life) on the video sleeve for *Soft Top*. Capaldi's film revolves around his character Gavin, a children's book illustrator struggling to make ends meet in the bright lights of London. Randomly, he bumps into his Uncle Salvatore in a bar, played by another Scot, Richard Wilson OBE (probably best known as the nation's favourite misanthrope Victor Meldrew, in the hugely popular BBC comedy series *One Foot in the Grave*).

It is Salvatore who informs Gavin that his father has just sold the Scots/Italian ice cream business. To claim his share, he must return immediately to his family home in Glasgow for his father's birthday. Without delay he leaves a gridlocked city behind in a dusted-off 'Crazyhorse' his light blue, K-reg Triumph Herald convertible. Heading north on a journey fraught with problems, he stops at Lancaster Services (formerly named Forton), a familiar landmark for those who regularly travel to and from Cumbria, between Junctions 32-33 on the M6. Here he picks up a hitch-hiker named Yvonne

(Collins) who turns out to be carrying a handy secret with her.

The service station was designed by architects T. P. Bennett & Son, and opened in January 1965 fully embracing the American style of dining and refreshment. The design signified a bullish spirit enveloping the whole country, as the new motorways started to make their presence felt in the countryside. Built and operated by the Top Rank Organisation, some of its earliest customers reputedly included the Fab Four, who made the 70-mile journey from Liverpool to experience the dawn of a modern world full of speed and late-night cappuccinos. What made the services so distinctive was a 65 feet high tower (subsequently dubbed The Pennine Tower), which housed a 120-seat restaurant with waiter service, topped by an open deck sun terrace – a noble idea round those parts! In the film, Yvonne refers to the tall structure as 'a sleeping giant that must have been really something in its day.' Nowadays the tower has been mothballed, with the restaurant long gone and most of the original fittings removed. However, the building remains a landmark to thousands of motorists, due to it becoming a Grade II listed building in 2012.

The film's only Cumbrian location can be glimpsed when Gavin and Yvonne drive past the Ship Inn pub and restaurant situated at Sandside on the B5282 between Milnthorpe and Arnside. A place with an unrivalled prospect, it offers travellers spectacular views over the Milnthorpe sands on the Kent estuary and across to the distant Coniston fells. With the imposing limestone cliffs of Whitbarrow scar rearing up in the immediate foreground.

The Ship Inn, Sandside, near Milnthorpe.

Sandside near Milnthorpe, LA7 7HW. Grid ref: SD 48028 80962.

Soldiers of the Damned

Mark Nuttall, 2015

'An Evil Secret Awaits'

Certificate: 18
Producers: Nigel Horne, Stephen Rigg
Photography: James Martin
Cast: Gil Darnell, Miriam Cooke, Lucas Hansen, Tom Sawyer
Colour: 99 minutes
Screenplay: Nigel Horne
Music: Tug

Greystoke Castle Estate doubles for a Romanian forest in a supernatural horror thriller set in World War II. The film's script was the brainchild of first-time director Mark Nuttall, writer Nigel Horne and producer Stephen Rigg of Blackdog productions. Equity investors played a crucial part helping them to self-finance the project. They arrived at the decision to use Greystoke Forest as the main location after looking at fifteen other potential forests. It is now owned by M-Sport in Cockermouth, who use the forest for testing and setting up Ford Fiesta World Rally Cars. The production team soon developed a good working relationship with M-Sport, who became very keen for the film-makers to show off the forest and help advertise the area.

One of Cumbria's hidden gems, the castle's privately owned estate covers around 3,000 miles of mixed terrain and is situated on the north-eastern side of the Lake District near Penrith. Its name derives from Llyulph de Greystoke, who had originally constructed a wooden defensive pele tower soon after the Norman conquest of 1066. His grandson Ivo rebuilt it in stone in the early twelfth century. A couple of century's later William de Greystoke obtained Royal permission to turn the castle into a castellated classic. However, Oliver Cromwell had it destroyed in 1660 as a result of its allegiance to Charles I in the English civil war. For years it lay in ruins until Henry Howard eventually rebuilt and enlarged it in the Victorian era.

Throughout most of the Second World War the army commandeered the estate, turning it into a tank-drivers' training ground. Like Grizedale Hall (featured in *The One That Got Away*) a little further south, the castle was also used as a Prisoner of War camp, mainly for Polish soldiers fighting on the German side. More recently in August 2012, the castle hosted a special evening of jazz, cross-dressing and comedy for a fun-packed Picnic cinema screening of Billy Wilder's classic film *Some Like it Hot*.

Set at the end of the war in 1944, *Soldiers of the Damned* begins with Hitler's forces in retreat on the Eastern front. Russian soldiers have broken through German lines and successfully forced them back through Romania. Meanwhile, an elite group of Nazi troops led by a disillusioned Major Kurt Fleischer (Gil Darnell) are assigned an especially dangerous mission. Their orders are to escort a female scientist into a mysterious forest behind enemy lines in order to recover an ancient relic.

The blood-letting soon starts, when one by one the soldiers disappear after an unknown force begins to play with them psychologically. Forcing them to move through time into a parallel world as they plunge deeper into the forest. Eventually Fleischer realises Professor Anna Kappel (Miriam Cooke) is under direct orders from the notorious occult department set up by Himmler, leader of the feared SS. Yet despite this terrible discovery, it is still the possessed forest that presents the biggest danger to their increasingly blood-soaked assignment. The film's story bears a similar comparison with American director Michael Mann's (*Heat, Miami Vice*) brooding 1983 film *The Keep*. Which was also set in Romania and featured a large slice of Third Reich mysticism.

The main cast at Greystoke Forest © Blackdog Productions 2015

Assembling the cast took a long time, but after a year in development, shooting took place between April and May 2013 for four weeks at Greystoke Forest (including one day's filming at the castle provided by Neville Howard). They also used a barn in the small village of Newbiggin (about three miles from Penrith) as an interior location. Some of the most atmospheric scenes towards the film's climax were shot at the Hoffman limekiln tunnel at Langcliffe in the Yorkshire Dales. Ironically, a German inventor Friedrich Hoffman patented the former kiln in 1858 – the kiln could produce lime in a continuous burning cycle. Once a key part of local industry with 22 chambers, it provides a suitably dark and shadowy atmosphere to match the gloomy cinematography of the forest.

Predictably, one of the most challenging aspects of the shoot proved to be the Cumbrian weather, which naturally threw everything at them. From sunshine, rain, hail and snow. Sometimes all at once in the space of a few seconds! The wet conditions also played havoc with the blood work of make-up artists administering flesh wounds. During filming the cast and crew stayed at the nearby Travelodge in Penrith and Newton Rigg College. The college also provided catering services, including breakfast and evening meals at the campus restaurant, whilst bringing lunches to the film set in Greystoke Forest. Despite the challenging conditions, producer Stephen Rigg remembers the shoot fondly, describing the experience of filming in the Lake District as a pleasure.

Included on the DVD release is an entertaining and informative 'Making of' featurette. Filmed in a documentary style, it highlights the otherwise unknown contribution made by military advisor, Ronnie Papaleo, (who'd previously worked on a handful of lavish WWII productions, including: *Atonement*, *Valkyrie* and *Charlotte Gray*). Based at Brampton near Carlisle, Papaleo and his company (K.R.U.S.) specialise in providing weapons and props, costumes and action vehicles for film and TV. The production team came to rely heavily on his considerable collection of Second World War memorabilia.

A number of cinemas in the North West hosted screenings in August 2015, prior to the film being made available by Safecracker Pictures on DVD and across all Digital platforms.

Greystoke, CA11 0TG. Grid ref: NY 43543089.

Star Wars: Episode VII – The Force Awakens

J. J. Abrams, 2015

Certificate: PG-13   Colour: 135 minutes
Producers: J. J. Abrams, Michael Arndt (associate), Bryan Burk, Leifur B. Dagfinnsson (line), Tommy Gormley (co), Tommy Harper (executive), Kathleen Kennedy, Jason D. McGatlin (executive), Michelle Rejwan (co), Ben Rosenblatt (co), John Swartz (co), Lawrence Kasdan (co – uncredited).
Screenplay: Lawrence Kasdan, J. J. Abrams, Michael Arndt
Photography: Daniel Mindel   Music: John Williams
Cast: Harrison Ford, Mark Hamill, Carrie Fisher, Adam Driver, Daisy Ridley, John Boyega, Oscar Isaac

In possibly the biggest blockbuster deal ever, the Walt Disney Company acquired the all-conquering *Star Wars* franchise at the end of October 2012. They immediately set about outlining plans for a third sequel trilogy with the first instalment, *Episode VII* to be released in December 2015. The world then waited on tenterhooks until November 2014 before getting a glimpse of how American director J. J. Abrams' (*Star Trek, Star Trek Into Darkness*) *The Force Awakens* was shaping up. A pair of teaser trailers ignited the hype, with the second teaser landing in April 2015 and receiving nearly 70 million views worldwide. Easily beating all-comers to become YouTube's most viewed trailer in 2015.

Somewhat unexpectedly, the opening salvo also created an awakening in Cumbria. Avid observers discovered the Force was strong in the Lake District after spotting three X-Wing fighters in the first teaser, (created using CGI and other effects) speeding across a smoldering Derwentwater. The distinctive outline of the iconic mountain Blencathra with Walla Crag to the fore completed a new magical piece of cinematic history for the region.

Reality then turned into fantasy in the second trailer, when another cluster of X-Wings were identified low-flying over Thirlmere. In a scene clearly reminiscent of how RAF fighter jets similarly tear through the skies on dangerously low fly-by training manoeuvres, in what has now become a common sight in the Lake District, often on a daily basis. With typical daring-do, the X-Wings spectacularly skim the water's surface within touching distance of the impressive slab of rock, known as Raven Crag. Staff at the Scafell Hotel in Borrowdale backed-up news of all this exciting footage; declaring a film crew had stayed there in the summer of 2014. Reports soon surfaced of a helicopter performing aerial shots as part of a small special effects team, which had been filming around the Manesty Park area of Derwentwater. These

X-wing fighters skimming across Derwentwater with Walla Crag in the distance, courtesy of Lucasfilm Ltd, LCC. Copyright Star Wars: The Force Awakens & Lucasfilm Ltd., LCC.

developments confirmed how the amazing teaser images had been filmed and promptly sent both social and local media into hyperspace.

Earlier Cumbrian connections with *Star Wars* include a number of similarities between Michael Anderson's classic 1955 film *The Dambusters* (also partly filmed in the Lake District) and the original *Episode IV: A New Hope* (created by George Lucas and released in 1977). These films shared the considerable talents of two late Englishmen, Gilbert Taylor who provided special effects photography on *The Dambusters* and cinematography on *Episode IV*. Like Taylor, make-up artist Stuart Freeborn also worked on both, before becoming part of the team behind the unique Yoda and Jabba the Hut puppets. It is widely thought Lucas borrowed heavily from the low-flying exploits first seen in *The Dambusters* along with the numerous cockpit scenes. All of which subsequently influenced how the action featuring X-Wing pilots or the gun-turrets of the Millennium Falcon were filmed. The battle to destroy the Death Star also had strong echoes of the Lancaster bombers' wave of attacks on the trio of German dams.

Like the original *Star Wars* trilogy, *Episode VII* was mainly filmed in the UK, but only this time at Pinewood Studios, along with a handful of other locations including, Greenham Common and the Forest of Dean. To the delight of older fans the cast had a more nostalgic feel to it with Mark Hamill, Carrie Fisher and Harrison Ford reprising the classic roles of Luke Skywalker, Princess Leia and Han Solo. Oscar Isaac (*Inside Llewyn Davis*), Adam Driver (*Frances Ha*), Max von Sydow (*Shutter Island*), John Boyega (*Attack the Block*) and Andy Serkis (*The Hobbit: An Unexpected Journey*) also joined the cast along with newcomers Daisy Ridley and Pip Andersen. During filming, Hollywood A-lister Harrison Ford even paid an impromptu visit to Cumbria when he dropped in at Carlisle Airport to refuel his helicopter.

With the fans ultimate experience, *Star Wars Celebration* holding court for four days at London's ExCel Exhibition Centre in July 2016. There is the distinct possibility of countless diehard fans attempting to seek out the film's UK locations. This will inevitably focus attention on Cumbria and encourage new pilgrimages to experience the dark and light landscape of where the X-Wings first made a splash in the Lake District.

Derwentwater (Manesty Park), CA12 5UG. Grid ref: NY 25600 19100.
Thirlmere, CA12 4TG. Grid ref: NY 30400 18700.

⁂

The Stars Look Down Carol Reid, 1939
'A Story of Simple Working People'

Certificate: PG   Black & White: 110 minutes
Producers: Isadore Goldsmith, Maurice J. Wilson
Screenplay: J. B. Williams (screenplay), A. J. Cronin (novel and adaptation), J. B. Williams (scenario), A. Coppel (scenario)
Cast: Michael Redgrave, Margaret Lockwood   Music: Hans May

Dr Finlay's Casebook is remembered today as one of the most popular TV series produced for the BBC in the 1960s. It spawned much loved characters such as Andrew Cruikshank and Barbara Mullen who became household names. Both were the creation of Scottish author, A. J. Cronin, who based them on his own experiences as a doctor at a modest village on the Clyde, and in Tredegar, a mining town in South Wales. It was during his role as a Medical Inspector for the Mines of Great Britain, that he bore witness to many distressing scenes in a disaster at Ystfad Colliery, Pengelly. Tragically, 38 miners lost their lives, whilst the remaining 23 were eventually rescued.

Later in life, he would draw on this haunting experience when penning, *The Citadel* and *The Stars Look Down*, both novels written about the inherent dangers faced by miners. He also wrote the screenplay for the film version of *The Stars Look Down*, where director Carol Reed (*The Third Man*) portrayed aspects of the injustices found in working conditions and labour relations at a North East mining community. The film starred a very young looking Michael Redgrave (*The Dambusters*) as Davey Fenwick, a man on the up who leaves the family home against his mother's wishes after gaining a scholarship to university. Although he still hopes to return and help the miners in their ongoing battle against unsafe working conditions.

Whilst studying, he falls in love and marries Jenny Sunley (Margaret Lockwood) a manipulative, materialistic girl who desires social acceptance above family values. Both Redgrave and Lockwood had just become stars playing the attractive couple, Gilbert and Iris in Hithcock's *The Lady*

Vanishes, a witty tale of espionage released in 1938. Made on the eve of the Second World War *The Stars Look Down* highlights a confrontation between gritty social realism and expanding capitalist greed. Filmed despite the onset of war, it must have been an incredibly brave film for a relatively small production company to undertake. Worldwide events didn't deter the exiled Austrian producer, Isidore Goldsmith, who'd taken over Grafton Films in the mid-1930s. Goldsmith had somehow managed to raise £100,000, an extraordinary amount to finance such a project at the time.

This substantial backing enabled Reed to film on location, as shooting began just a stone's throw away from the Irish Sea at the former Great Clifton and St. Helens collieries, situated north of Workington, near to the village of Siddick.

Another seven weeks filming at Denham and Twickenham Studios, followed, where they re-constructed the Cumbrian pit-head (made-up of an incredible 40,000 square yards). In its time it became the largest exterior set ever made in British film. The exact replica of the pithead also included rows of miner's cottages, along with pieces of clothing bought from colliery workers, together with pit ponies from Cumbria, brought-in especially to ensure complete authenticity. Reed used three camera crews on the set before it was eventually moved to Shepperton Studios, Surrey, for the final bits of filming.

There are records of a mining disaster on 19 April 1888 at St. Helens Colliery, which closely resemble some of the tragic scenes in the film's climax.

The film poster featuring Redgrave & Lockwood, © Grafton Films, 1939.

Except in the real catastrophe, water was used to flood the mines, helping to extinguish underground flames set alight by a shot fire. Sadly, thirty men and twelve pit ponies lost their lives, despite numerous volunteers mounting a rescue mission, just as they try to do in the film.

Siddick near Workington, CA14 1LA. Grid ref: NY 00050 31199.

Swallows and Amazons
Claude Whatham, 1974 and Philippa Lowthorpe, 2016
'One of the best-loved children's stories of all time'

Certificate: U   Colour: 92 minutes
Producers: Richard Pilbrow, Neville C. Thompson (associate)
Screenplay: David Wood, Arthur Ransome (novel)
Photography: Dennis C. Lewiston   Music: Wilfred Josephs
Cast: Virginia McKenna, Ronald Fraser, Simon West, Suzanna Hamilton, Sophie Neville, Stephen Grendon, Kit Seymour, Leslie Bennett

It still seems incredible that there isn't a designated visitor attraction dedicated to Arthur Ransome in the Lake District. Especially given the enormous influence that his stories have had on generations of children since the 1930s. Surely the author of the twelve *Swallows and Amazons* series of books deserves a seat at the same literary banquet served up by Beatrix Potter and William Wordsworth. Hope remains in the shape of the Arthur Ransome Trust, which has been trying to establish a centre devoted to his work for a number of years.

Until recently, Ransome's enduring adventures were also kept alive by British director Claude Whatham's hugely successful film that compliments the books perfectly. To celebrate the 40th anniversary of the film's release in 1974, a whole new generation of fans were treated to a re-badged digitally restored edition released on DVD and Blu-Ray in 2014. A year later, the much-loved classic finally got the green light to a slightly controversial 21st Century makeover by Harbour Pictures and BBC Films. Despite encountering numerous pre-production delays, shooting began at Coniston and Derwentwater in June 2015 before moving on to film in Yorkshire. With the role of Jim Turner (aka retired pirate Captain Flint) going to Rafe Spall, son of Timothy Spall OBE, who ironically played *Mr Turner* in Mike Leigh's critically acclaimed 2014 biopic.

A strong British cast also featured Kelly Macdonald (*Brave*) as Mrs Walker, *Game of Thrones* actress Gwendoline Christie as Mrs Blackett, with the TV comedic duo Harry Enfield and Jessica Hynes as Mr and Mrs Jackson.

the TV comedic duo Harry Enfield and Jessica Hynes as Mr and Mrs Jackson. In one of the least contentious changes from the original story, Andrew Scott (best known as Jim Moriarty in the BBC series *Sherlock*) played a new character, the mysterious secret agent called Lazlow. The screenplay by Scottish film and television writer Andrea Gibb had clearly been inspired by Ransome's secret life as a spy. Where he reported on the Russian revolution for the British intelligence service MI6 until fleeing Russia with Trotsky's secretary. They reached the Baltic in 1924 and later married.

Despite Harbour Pictures claiming that their updated version would remain faithful to the original story, a decision to alter the name of one of the main characters provoked a great deal of debate. The furore started after word leaked out that Able Seaman Titty Walker would become Tatty Walker in the new film. A spokesman for the BBC quickly denied it had been changed for politically correct reasons. The outcry in some of the National newspapers prompted one to question where it would end if all double-entendre's were banned. Perhaps it is not that much of an amendment though, as Ransome had originally taken inspiration from watching his friends' five children sail on Coniston Water. Their names were Taqui, Susie, Titty and Roger along with Brigit the ship's baby. Titty's real name was Mavis, but she hated it and was given the family nickname adopted from the tale of *Titty Mouse and Tatty Mouse* written by Joseph Jacobs.

It is not the first time Titty's name has been changed, however, as in a 1963 TV adaptation for the BBC, they renamed her character Kitty, played by Susan George. Although Ransome never clearly indicated who inspired the characters of Nancy and Peggy Blackett, a woman from Coniston, (the late Pauline Marshall known as Paulie) always claimed that she and her elder sister Georgie were the real Amazons. As a young girl she often played with her sister on or around the shores of Coniston Water. She believed it was through witnessing their sailing adventures that Ransome's imagination would have been stirred to invent the pirate loving tomboys.

Thankfully, in the new adaptation, the other names of the Walker and Blackett children remain unchanged. They were played by a handful of breakthrough stars including, Dane Hughes as John Walker, Orla Hill as Susan Walker, Teddie-Rose Malleson-Allen as the aforementioned Tatty Walker, Bobby McCulloch as Roger Walker, with Seren Hawkes as Nancy Blackett and Hannah Jayne Thorp from Burneside, near Kendal as her sister, Peggy. Appropriately, the production also included a number of other locals after Carlisle-based Lakeside Casting Agency worked tirelessly to provide enough male extras willing to have a short-back-and-sides hair cut. The Glenridding Sailing Centre (which normally has moorings at Ullswater) supplied two of its replica Lune Whammel coastal fishing boats for filming on Derwentwater. During the shoot a number of highly visible magenta coloured signs were posted around the lake, serving as guides to the locations. Location number

Location sign leading to Plattyplus, Derwentwater.

two was located at Plattyplus, a small family run water sports business situated on the shores of Derwentwater opposite the Lodore Falls Hotel.

The company usually offer visitors the chance to try out a Viking-style longboat, action-packed dragon boating or just bobbing around the lake in a kayak or a canoe. But for two weeks in early July 2015, their jetty was used as a base for filming, where the British Canoe Union qualified staff provided assistance and safety tips throughout. Fortunately, filming took place in near perfect conditions, as the cast and crew enjoyed some of the hottest weather of the year.

Whatham's enchanting and relatively faithful recreation for Anglo EMI had been filmed almost exclusively on location in the Lake District during the summer term (May-July) of 1973. It was eventually released with a U certificate on 4 April 1974. David Wood (dubbed 'the national children's dramatist' by Irvine Wardle in *The Times*) wrote the original screenplay, and adapted the book for BBC Radio 4. The film is thought to have provided the catalyst for families across the UK to start flocking to the Lake District, to seek out the same places where the four children had their adventures.

Incredibly, as a six week old baby, Ransome had been carried to the summit of the Old Man of Coniston during his first trip to the Lake District. Throughout his childhood he spent summer holidays on or around the foot of Coniston Water, before he was sent to a prep school in Windermere. Even as a young man, and later in his 30s and 40s when working as a foreign correspondent for the *Manchester Guardian*, he would aim to return to The

Lakes every summer, to go walking or to write. His most successful book is directly inspired by recollections of his early holidays at Coniston, particularly those at the Swainson's Farm near the southern end of the lake in Nibthwaite.

As a young man he also spent considerable time nearby at Lanehead – the family home of W. G. Collingwood, Ruskin's former secretary and biographer. Collingwood became a major influence on him, encouraging the young Ransome to write and take up sailing. In *Swallows and Amazons* Ransome incorporated a number of places he sailed to or camped at throughout his life, such as Peel Island on Coniston Water, which subsequently became known as Wild Cat Island in the book, even though the landing place and tall pine tree lighthouse are likely to have been Blake Holme on Windermere.

Allan Tarn, a water lily covered pool close to the mouth of the River Crake near Nibthwaite, was renamed Octopus Lagoon. Famously, the timeless adventure was written for W. G.'s daughter, Dora Altounyan's (née Collingwood) five children, in exchange for a pair of bright red Turkish slippers! These can be seen at the excellent Lakeland Arts Museum of Lakeland Life in Kendal.

For the original film version, Whatham wanted a cast made up of children who hadn't attended stage school, but who could row a boat and were ideally members of sailing clubs. The four 'Swallows' chosen as the Walker family children included: Suzanna Hamilton as Susan, Simon West as John, Stephen Grendon as Roger and Sophie Neville as Titty.

Director Claude Whatham shares a joke with the crew of Swallow at Derwentwater, ©1974 Studio Canal Films Ltd.

The 'Amazons' were played by Kit Seymour as Nancy Blackett and Lesley Bennett as her sister Peggy. Virginia McKenna, a classic English heroine of films such as (*Carve Her Name with Pride, A Town Like Alice* and *The Cruel Sea*) starred as Mrs Walker. Her soft tones also graced the enchanting film *(Born Free,* 1966*)*, alongside her husband Bill Travers, and Elsa the lion cub. Now aged in her eighties, McKenna still looks back fondly on *Swallows and Amazons* for the 2014 DVD re-issue, claiming the film depicts a time of lost innocence where children were allowed the freedom to have fun. The late Ronald Fraser (*The Flight of the Phoenix*) filled the other adult role of the Blacketts' Uncle Jim, aka Captain Flint (named after the character in Robert Louis Stevenson's *Treasure Island*). Out of all the children, only Suzanna Hamilton went on to feature in a number of other films. One of her most notable roles was playing Julia opposite John Hurt and Richard Burton in Michael Radford's sombre adaption of George Orwell's seminal novel *1984*. A year later she played the part of Felicity in Sydney Pollack's multi-Oscar winning *Out of Africa*.

Sophie Neville has since recounted many of her experiences playing the role of Titty in a series of wonderfully entertaining books, culminating with *The Making of Swallows and Amazons,* published to coincide with the film's 40th anniversary. These fascinating reminiscences include a first-hand account into all the wet, gloomy days on set from her original diary. There are also a large amount of behind the scenes photographs, maps, excerpts from the script and a huge amount of invaluable information and secrets for fans of the film.

Rather fittingly, Neville's multifaceted career included a spell casting the children for the 1984 BBC TV serial, *Swallows and Amazons Forever!* an adaptation of Arthur Ransome's books, *Coot Club* and *The Big Six*, set on the Norfolk Broads. Locations for Whatham's film included Haverthwaite Station at the southern end of Windermere on the A590 near Newby Bridge. Bank Ground Farm on the eastern shores of Coniston Water was used as 'Holly Howe' the name given by Ransome for the fictional holiday home of the Walker family, where the Altounyan children stayed themselves in 1928. It is a Grade II listed traditional farmhouse dating back to the fifteenth century, with low ceilings; oak beams and open log fires. For the last fifty years or so it has been providing bed and breakfast accommodation.

Whatham and Richard Pilbrow (the producer) chose the iconic viewpoint of Friar's Crag on Derwentwater for the Peak of Darien location. In the book, the children are having a picnic there when Captain John receives the 'if not duffers' telegram from their absent father. However, one of the film's biggest secrets is contained in the scene where they run up to the Peak for their very first glimpse of Wild Cat Island. According to Neville, this marks the only scene filmed outside the Lake District. It was actually shot under an oak tree in Runnymede, near the River Thames – a place more associated with King

Sophie Neville's hand-drawn map of Coniston Water, © Sophie Neville.

Bank Ground Farm, Coniston.

John, and the signing of Magna Carta some 800 years ago.

Almost all the scenes on Wild Cat Island were filmed at Peel Island on Coniston, as Pilbrow had been disappointed by the sight of caravans near to the shore when scouting Blake Holme on Windermere a year before shooting commenced. The 'secret harbour' on the west side of Peel Island is now a Mecca for *Swallows and Amazons* enthusiasts the world over who can hire a boat or canoe from the Coniston Boating Centre in order to explore its perimeter or surrounding landscape. To film the sailing sequences, the production crew built a cross-shaped 30-foot raft (referred to as a 'pontoon') equipped with two outboard engines and flat boards, so that Whatham could shoot from a number of different angles.

They got around the problem of filming night-time scenes by shooting

'Swallow' lashed to the camera pontoon on Coniston © Sophie Neville.

Swallows and Amazons fishing on a makeshift jetty upon Derwentwater with Ronald Fraser, © Sophie Neville.

them in broad daylight with 'day-for-night' lenses on the cameras, to make it look like they were set at night. Art Director, Simon Holland had a busy time trying to make the streets around Bowness Bay of 1973 look like a quaint Lakeland town in 1929. The Swallows refer to Bowness as the native settlement 'Rio Bay' after believing the Amazons have dropped anchor there. John, Susan and Titty come ashore to visit a general store (really a garage dressed up as a 1920s 'native' chandlery, which is now a barber's shop). They buy rope for the lighthouse tree and four bottles of grog (ginger beer) before walking past the Stags Head Hotel on Church Street – now one of the most popular destinations for visitors to the Lake District.

On a journey to Wild Cat Island, the Swallows nearly collide with a beautiful Lakeland passenger steamer called *Tern*, a special piece of Victorian opulence in service since 1891. The fishing scene where Roger tries to catch a huge, fearsome pike was filmed away from Coniston at a reedy bay on Elterwater. Another of the production secrets revealed by Neville involves the night scenes on Wild Cat Island, which were actually shot inside the barn at Bank Ground. Apparently Whatham had no choice in the matter, due to the wet weather conditions they encountered. Set dresser Ian Whittaker (who went on to win two Oscars) had the considerable task of turning the barn into an island camp, replete with a fire, blankets and pillows.

The children come face to face with an adder and an old Lakeland tradition when they pay a visit to a charcoal burners' hut at Grizedale forest, situated above Coniston water. John, Susan and Roger are at the helm on board *Swallow* when they find Titty with the captured *Amazon* anchored near Cormorant Island, filmed at Lingholm Island on Derwentwater, (despite Ransome admitting that the island was based on Silver Holme on Windermere).

Brown Howe cottage, once part of the Duke of Buccleuch's summer estate, close to Torver on the southern banks of Coniston Water, was used as the location for Beckfoot, the Amazons' home. Built in 1925, the *Lady Derwentwater* is a 56-foot vessel capable of carrying 90 passengers for cruises on Derwentwater; in the film it had the starring role of Captain Flint's houseboat. Although she looked a little different from the *SY Esperance*, the vessel Ransome had in mind, but her large cabin windows gave Claude Whatham wonderful views out over the lake.

In April 2010, *Swallow,* one of the dinghies used in the film was sold at auction. A group of 80 dedicated fans clubbed together to buy the unique vintage boat, raising awareness and donating to an appeal. Having secured it, Ransome fans from around the UK and beyond have since been able to experience sailing adventures 'in which the boundaries between the real and the imagined grow thin, and wonder spreads over both.'

Coniston, LA21 8EZ. Grid ref: SD 30077 97323.
Haverthwaite, LA12 8AE. Grid ref: SD 34105 83935.
Derwentwater (Plattyplus), CA12 5UX. Grid ref: NY 26435 18870.
Elterwater, LA22 9HW. Grid ref: NY 32918 04780.
The Stags Hotel, Bowness, LA23 3DG. Grid ref: SD 40235 96928.
Grizedale, LA22 0QU. Grid ref: SD 33571 94386.

T

Three and Out Jonathan Gershfield, 2008
'A Deal is a Deal'

Certificate: 15   Colour: 106 minutes
Producers: Aaron Gershfield (executive), Wayne Marc Godfrey, Mark Gottlieb (associate), Ian Harries, Tim Johnson (associate), Paul Sarony (line), Gordon Synn (associate)
Screenplay: Steve Lewis, Tony Owen   Photography: Richard Greatrex
Music: Trevor Jones
Cast: MacKenzie Crook, Colm Meaney, Imelda Staunton, Gemma Arterton

A film that came with a big fanfare and huge marketing spend, but ended up almost heralding the demise of the so-called 'Britcom'. Lead actor MacKenzie Crook, had originally sprung to fame playing Gareth Keenan in the BBC TV series, *The Office,* a multi-award winning Mockumentary; created, written and directed by Ricky Gervais and Stephen Merchant. However, years later, (without naming names), Gervais delivered a clear rebuke to some of his former co-stars, claiming comedians who suddenly gain success often make a handful of tacky, dismal flops that go straight to DVD. Who knows whether he was referring to the debut 2008 offering from British director Jonathan Gershfield which boasted a strong cast including the dependable pairing of Colm Meaney and Imelda Staunton along with a fine cameo appearance from the stunning Gemma Arterton.

In the film, Crook plays Paul Callow, a depressed tube driver on the London Underground, who hears of the 'three and out' rule after accidently striking dead two pedestrians in the space of a week. The un-written law states any driver who kills three people in a month is entitled to a ten year pay-off on full salary to help cope with the psychological damage. Callow quickly views this macabre policy as an opportunity to change his life for the better. Eventually his search for a willing suicide to assist him leads to an Irish drunkard, Tommy Cassidy (Meaney).

Cassidy agrees to oblige, but only if two conditions are met. The first involves Callow handing over a large amount of money and the second sees him accompany Cassidy on a road trip to the Lake District where he hopes to make peace with his estranged wife Rose (Staunton) and daughter, Frankie (Arterton).

The Miner's Bridge, Coniston.

After their arrival in the Lake District they start to ascend the precipitous Wrynose Pass in a retro Mercedes car sporting a fitting number plate – 430 OUT. The scenes at Rosemary and Frankie's small white cottage were filmed at a house in a characteristic row near the Ruskin Museum and Black Bull pub on Yewdale Road, Coniston. After spending the night with Frankie, Callow is discovered in her bedroom the following morning by Cassidy who chases him out of the house to the Miners Bridge over Church Beck above Coniston.

A brief skirmish ensues before Cassidy collapses and is taken away by ambulance to the Village Institute's old library, which doubled as a hospital. The building inspired by the life and work of John Ruskin, reopened its doors in 2012 after undergoing a full renovation thanks to the combined efforts of local residents and the Grizedale Arts organisation. It now houses a new library, kitchens, indoor markets, reading room and even a community-run 'honesty shop'.

The film is perhaps remembered more for courting controversy with the train drivers' union Aslef, who handed out leaflets to moviegoers at its Leicester square premiere, protesting about the perceived trivialisation of railway deaths. They also voiced concerns with London Underground for letting the film-makers use their facilities, whilst suggesting that they had showed 'contempt' for union members at the same time. A claim embellished by Gershfield and his producer Wayne Marc Godfrey, who openly admitted to hyping-up ASLEF's protests in the film's marketing campaign, which ultimately proved fruitless at the box office.

Coniston, LA21 8DU. Grid ref: SD 30202 97666.

AN A TO Z: CUMBRIA AND THE LAKE DISTRICT ON FILM

27 Memory Lane   Luke Hupton, 2014

'A love that is lived, is never lost'

Producer: Luke Hupton
Screenplay: Luke Hupton
Music: Mark Daniel Dunnett
Cast: James Clay, Dani Harrison, Michael Maughan
Colour: 98 minutes
Photography: Ed Lambert

The streets of Sedbergh and nearby small hamlet of Millthrop feature in writer and filmmaker Luke Hupton's memorable debut romantic fantasy. The story is centred on the life of August Pennyworth, a middle-aged divorced general practitioner, who has been living under a cloud after abandoning the only woman he ever loved when he was 27-years-old. At the beginning of the film August receives the curious gift of an antique door as a result of an incident at Yorkshire Dales Antiques (formerly known as Memory Lane Antiques) a hidden gem for collectibles in Sedbergh.

It arrives after he bravely chases a pair of thieves wearing balaclavas through the narrow main street to rescue a stolen ornament. Running passed a shop named 'Sleepy Elephant' along the way. A title that refers to a comment made by A. Wainwright who likened the Howgill Fells to a 'huddle of squatting elephants'. When August eventually fits the door to his home it magically leads to a cobbled street that appears lost in time. Returning back to his 27th year, he soon embarks on a quest to unravel the haunting secrets of his life in the hope of finding the one girl he truly loved.

Completed on a miniscule budget of £15,000 the film also included a cast and crew assembled from all corners of the UK. James Clay (*My Week with Marilyn*) headed the cast as a younger August, whilst Michael Maughan played him aged 52. The striking actress and musician Dani Harrison played Paige Healey, August's former love. Aged only in his mid-twenties himself, Hupton originally gained the confidence to become a director after attending a hugely beneficial course on filmmaking at Salford College. He also cites the work of legendary auteur Alfred Hitchcock and his protégé Peter Bogdanovich as having played a major influence on him. Inspiration behind an intriguing storyline came from a desire to explore re-living a moment in someone's life from a different perspective. In this case with the benefit of age and the supposed maturity gained from it.

Hupton opted to film in Sedbergh for its quiet beauty and chocolate box-type qualities. Whilst on location there, he became indebted to the considerable help of Sue West (owner of the antique shop seen at the beginning) who let them film inside her store. She also showed him other potential locations nearby, which led to him using the small village of Millthrop. West also provided the perfect spot for the crucial final scene of the movie. Using her knowledge of the local landscape and influence with a farmer, who readily gave his permission for them to film on a rare hilltop displaying just one lonely tree. Throughout their time spent in Cumbria, Hupton became overwhelmed by the kindness shown to them. Even the local vicar opened up the church hall so they could use it as a base.

Whilst filming in Sedbergh, an extraordinary incident even made its way into the national press. It happened when an ex-policeman walked out of a dental practice mid-shot and wandered unknowingly into the robbery sequence. Assuming it was for real, he immediately tackled one of the actor's playing a masked robber. After pinning him to a wall, the ex-special ops man claimed he was acting purely on instinct, until Hupton ran over to explain the situation!

August, Evelyn and Peggy search for lost love in the middle of Millthrop, © Luke Hupton, 27 Memory Lane, 2014.

The Cumbrian village of Millthrop features towards the end when August closes in on his sweetheart along with his trusted friend Evelyn and Peggy (a very cute West Highland terrier, and apparently the source of great amusement on set). The film is made even more remarkable for the fact that Hupton was diagnosed with Obsessive Compulsive Disorder not long before shooting began, meaning he had to cope with the pressures of making the film whilst trying to cope with the intrusive thoughts he was suffering from throughout.

With the advent of the Industrial Revolution several mills sprang up around Sedbergh in the eighteenth century. Today, the remaining clusters of houses at Millthrop (which August wanders through) are a reminder of these times, having been originally built to house workers from the nearby cotton mill built in 1796. Trouble at the mills began after the outbreak of World War One, as the effects of other countries setting up their own factories to produce cheaper cloth, meant demand for British cotton slumped. At Sedbergh, (and throughout the rest of the UK), mills started to close down leaving Millthrop as the only viable one until it burned down in a spectacular fire in 1967.

There is still one remaining survivor of this period, situated just down the road on the fringes of Sedbergh, Farfield Mill is a former Victorian woollen mill that ceased production in the early 1990s. The building had fallen into a rather sorry state of disrepair, but was thankfully rescued from dereliction by a group of volunteers. It eventually emerged as an arts and crafts heritage centre, opening in April 2001. These days visitors from around the world can now feast themselves on a vibrant exhibition programme along with four levels of studios, galleries and heritage displays.

Sedbergh, LA10 5BL. Grid ref: SD 65744 92134.
Millthrop, LA10 5SL. Grid ref: SD 66231 91261.

28 Days Later   Danny Boyle, 2002
'The Days are numbered'

Certificate: 18   Colour: 113 minutes
Producers: Robert How (line), Andrew MacDonald
Screenplay: Alex Garland   Photography: Anthony Dod Mantle
Music: John Murphy
Cast: Cillian Murphy, Naomie Harris, Brendan Gleeson, Christopher Eccleston

One of only a handful of films released by the franchise DNA, a National Lottery funded company formed in 1997. Back then; the new Labour Government led by Tony Blair had invited the UK film industry to bid for what *Variety Magazine* dubbed, 'the great British Lottery circus.' In the blink of a zombie's eye, a number of franchises were quickly set up to try and breathe life into what had become an ailing industry. However, they proved to be highly controversial; big on promise, but lacking in delivery. DNA itself requested £29 million of funding to make sixteen films over six years – only releasing six.

Eventually DNA initiated a joint venture with Fox Searchlight (a sister company of the US major studio 20th Century Fox) to produce and distribute British films worldwide. One of DNA's co-founders, the producer Andrew MacDonald, who collaborated with director Danny Boyle on *Shallow Grave* (1994) and *Trainspotting* (1996) hoped that the release of *28 Days Later* would herald a successful partnership with Fox Searchlight and bring distinctive British films to a wider international audience.

The film is based on a post-apocalyptic thriller written by Alex Garland (who wrote *The Beach,* also adapted and directed by Boyle in 2000*)*. A virus called 'rage' is unleashed on Britain's unsuspecting population. The disease proves to be highly contagious, turning people into marauding zombies, who murder anyone near enough by literally ripping them apart. It stars Naomie Harris (Selena), Cillian Murphy (Jim) and Brendan Gleeson (Frank) who play three survivors, the so-called 'not infected.'

Boyle was apparently so keen to cast Harris in the film that he called her at home before her last audition. Advising that a tougher attitude and colder outlook was needed for Selena's character; definitely not the Princess Anne hairdo and posh accent she'd turned up to previous castings with! Boyle chose the remote, and peaceful setting of Ennerdale Water, the most westerly of all the lakes, as the setting for the end of the world. Situated in one of Cumbria's wildest valleys, it remains mostly inaccessible and relatively untouched.

Bowness Cottage, Bowness Knott, Ennerdale.

Without a public road around the lake, the majestic outlines of Pillar Mountain and Steeple continue to soar in relative isolation above the head of the water. At the end of the film, Selina, Hannah (Frank's teenage daughter) and Jim manage to escape via a deserted M6 motorway to Bowness Cottage at Bowness Knott, beside the soft lapping ripples caressing the lonely lakeshore. The final few sequences include a sweeping panorama of the eight-mile circuit round the lake, whilst Selina and Hannah unfurl a large stitched together cloth banner. Its message curiously spells out the word 'HELLO', as they attempt to attract the attentions of a jet fighter hurtling past overhead.

Bowness Knott, Ennerdale, CA23 3AU. Grid ref: NY 10274 16217.

W

We're Here for a Good Time, Not a Long Time   Kerry Harrison, 2014
'A Story of Love, Loss and a List'

Certificate: 15
Producers: David Gledhill, Kerry Harrison
Screenplay: David Gledhill
Music: Andy Duggan
Cast: Sam Allen, Kelly Wenham, Simon Atherton

Colour: 72 minutes

Photography: Kerry Harrison

The film's title is derived from a mantra that writer and director David Gledhill's partner Tracey tried to live her life by. Sadly, towards the end of her fifteen year battle with cystic fibrosis this saying became ever more poignant. Apparently, up until the last moments when she died aged 47, Tracey openly encouraged talking about death. She claimed it was the greatest gift you can ever have. Gledhill sat down and started writing as a way of coping when they both knew she was dying. In December 2011, after just ten days he had finished penning a script.

After Tracey's death a few months later in April, making the film eventually became a way for him to deal with the numbness of her loss. The story, clearly a labour of love follows an introverted main character David (played by Sam Allen) on a journey through the Lake District. David's character mostly meanders along in a 1960s VW camper van a year after his partner has passed away. The Lake District scenes are intermingled with a number of therapy sessions, which were filmed in an old Vicarage near Harrogate, North Yorkshire. Showing off some of the Lake District's most iconic landscape throughout November 2012, there are 22 locations resplendent with lush autumnal tones. The film was made with a minuscule budget of £10,000 over a period of just twelve days.

Gledhill, who had achieved modest success in a band with Tracey, turned to an old musician friend (now an advertising photographer) Kerry Harrison for directorial duties. Originally the script was set in the Scottish Highlands, but Harrison believed the Lakes would provide them with a much cheaper alternative. He also thought the foreboding skies and incredible muted; yet

Opening title, © *Kerry Harrison.*

rich colours of late autumn would be perfect. They eventually arrived in the Lake District at the onset of winter with a crew of just six people. A typically hospitable and Cumbrian welcome greeted them, which included free use of pubs, B&Bs and a boat on Derwentwater. Most of the scenes in the film were filmed in or around Keswick.

 The cast and crew stayed on the outskirts of town in a large house on Grange Park for the duration of the shoot, which also doubled as a location for a 30th birthday party. A memorable opening scene features the camper van driving along the Honister Pass in gloomy conditions with heavy sheets of rain falling sideways. Harrison said they had three cameras set up at various points to make sure they got all the footage needed in one take. The prospect of getting the van back up the Pass was simply not an option! Another vehicle had difficulties when the door from a hired Mercedes Splitter van came off when they attempted to film the scene. It had been literally wrenched from its hinges due to the strength of the winds!

 David spends his first night in the Lake District at Dalebottom Farm Caravan and Camping site in the Naddle Valley, two and a half miles south of Keswick. He first meets the other lead character Liz (Kelly Wenham) in a lay-by on the A591 near Thirlmere. They become friends after she spots him taking his cute little chihuahua (comically named Barry) for a walk outside her B&B – filmed at the Avondale in Southey Street, Keswick. Throughout the rest of the film David fights a natural attraction to Liz, as he remains very reluctant to allow himself to be happy. He buys some chips and takes Barry for a spontaneous and exceptionally wet boat ride on the Derwentwater steamers. He also takes him for numerous walks around the Keswick streets of Church Street, Leonard Street and St Johns Street. After showing up at Liz's friend's rather strange and sterile birthday party they go for a drive to the shores of Derwentwater again.

Other locations included an improvised passage at a fireworks display in Kendal and a moving coastal scene filmed just off the B5300 between Maryport and Allonby. Here, David finally attempts to move on by spreading his soulmate's ashes into the sea. The therapy sessions reveal that his partner tried to help him through the first year of her passing by writing him a list. This contained the idea for the trip and all of David's subsequent actions in the film. At the beginning there is an awkward moment at a remote petrol station (with two American style pumps) where David's isolation and social exclusion is particularly highlighted. Harrison said he found the perfect spot for this scene near to Ullswater. Needless to say he became very anxious that he would be able to use it. Luckily, he needn't have worried! For the owner had been an extra in Bruce Robinson's cult movie *Withnail and I* and couldn't wait to tell them all about it whilst they filmed! Fittingly, on the third anniversary of Tracey's death the film was made available online for free streaming on Vimeo.

Keswick, CA12 4NA. Grid ref: NY 26794 23492.
Honister Pass, CA12 5XJ. Grid ref: NY 21336 14167

Withnail and I   Bruce Robinson, 1987

'You are invited to spend a hilarious weekend in the English countryside'

Certificate: 15   Colour: 107 minutes
Producers: George Harrison (executive), Paul M. Heller, Lawrence Kirstein (associate), Denis O'Brien (executive), David Wimbury (co)
Screenplay: Bruce Robinson   Photography: Peter Hannan
Music: David Dundas, Rick Wentworth
Cast: Richard E. Grant, Paul McGann, Richard Griffiths, Ralph Brown, Michael Elphick

Undoubtedly still one of the best-known and seminal films to have been filmed in Cumbria. Bruce Robinson's semi-autobiographical classic low budget comedy still continues to enjoy a huge cult following almost 30 years on from its release. Initially a real slow-burner, the film only took around £500,000 at the UK box office when it first came out. However, it soon gained notoriety as a result of word-of-mouth recommendations by fans (particularly students) that often had to make do with watching it on murky VHS copies, long before a cleaned-up DVD version arrived in 2001. Despite featuring a cast of virtual unknowns and a first time director (Robinson), it nevertheless went on to take off in a most extraordinary way.

Set at the end of the 1960s, the film relays the story of two unemployed actors who live in a filthy, north London flat. Their wretched existence appears to consist solely of booze, pills and fags. Seeking a break from the overwhelming despair and squalor engulfing them, the pair bid farewell to London for a weekend in the country in an attempt to find some harmony and fresh air. The film catapulted Richard E. Grant to fame in his debut feature playing the hedonistic Withnail, along with a youthful Paul McGann as Marwood, his long suffering friend, known as the 'I' who is not named.

The late Shakespearean actor Richard Griffiths played the eccentric and ravenous homosexual, Uncle Monty, Withnail's relative who owns a dark, cold cottage tucked away in a remote corner of Cumbria. Over numerous glasses of sherry, Withnail persuades Monty to lend him the keys to the cottage known in the film as Crow Crag. Yet a supposed harmonious weekend in the country turns into a big mistake due to a mixture of inclement weather, no food, unfriendly locals, a randy bull and a mischievous poacher.

Uncle Monty's house, Crow Crag.

Their misery is finally realised when Monty turns up unexpectedly in the middle of the night, intent on throwing himself at a recoiling Marwood. Towards the end of the film, their descent into madness is almost complete when they smoke a huge spliff called a 'Camberwell Carrot.' The mind-numbing nine-skinner is rolled by the spaced out drug dealer Danny, played superbly by Ralph Brown, who resurrected the same character traits for the role of Del Preston a few years later in *Wayne's World 2* (1993).

As the film gained modern cult status, the Cumbrian locations became sites of pilgrimage to many hardcore fans, some of whom trekked from all over the world to visit them. Many die-hards have posted videos of their

The living room, above, and the courtyard, before refurbishment, 2013.

Oh my boys, my boys! Uncle Monty serves up a roast,
© AF archive/Alamy Stock Photo.

efforts paying homage on sites like YouTube, often attempting to recreate whole sequences from the film. Uncle Monty's cottage – Crow Crag, is really Sleddale Hall above the Wet Sleddale reservoir on the outskirts of Shap, a small village next to the M6 motorway. A former working farm, the eighteenth century cottage was initially owned by the Manchester Corporation from 1926 until being sold at auction by today's water board United Utilities in 2009.

Sadly, it had fallen into a state of dis-repair after filming took place and became badly in need of restoration. With open access and the chance to claim a keepsake for all those prepared to make the journey, it's easy to see why it also stood as a shrine for devotees. In the end (after the first deal fell through), the farmhouse was resold at auction for an undisclosed sum to Canterbury based architect, Tim Ellis in 2009, who then had to endure an 18-month wait before a planning application to turn the house into a family home was finally approved by the Lake District National Park Authority.

Ellis intended keeping original features such as floorboards and walls wherever possible, although the range in the kitchen (where Withnail and Marwood burn furniture to keep warm) had been removed about thirteen years before he moved in. In early 2013, some of the bright pink paint still survived on the bookshelves in the living room, the place in the film where they sit down to Uncle Monty's roast dinner.

Throughout the renovations Ellis slept in the kitchen, surviving without electricity in often freezing conditions, not too dissimilar to those encountered by the despairing duo in the film. When he moved in graffiti from fans keen to leave their imprint for posterity was still visible on some of the walls and beams. No doubt scribbled during numerous drunken escapades when the property was left entirely at the mercy of the Cumbrian weather. Since acquiring the property he has also consented to a number of special outdoor screenings of the film, organised by the hugely successful Eden Arts Picnic Cinema project. Held in the courtyard, these events instantly sell out, with 2013's screenings held in memory of the property's spiritual owner, Richard Griffiths aka Uncle Monty.

In 2015, more recognition followed for Withnail's gay uncle, when Sleddale Hall formed part of CELEBRATE: a new project designed to explore and uncover the living history of Cumbria's LGBT community.

Another location close to Crow Crag is the packhorse bridge over Sleddale beck, reached en route to the farmhouse if you walk around Wet Sleddale reservoir starting from the car park at the United Utilities dam. It was under the old stone bridge that a starving Withnail tried to shoot fish in the gushing pools, using the double-barrelled shotgun from Monty's kitchen. The striking view Marwood witnesses outside Crow Crag was actually shot at a different location, just down the road in the remote Mardale Valley, overlooking the Rigg on Haweswater.

This large reservoir had been controversially built by the Manchester Corporation after an act of Parliament granted them permission to start

The iconic phone box at Bampton.

construction in 1929 in order to supply water to the north-west of England. A whole community had been intentionally wiped off the map when all the farms and houses of the villages of Mardale and Measand, along with the local Dun Bull Inn were flooded and lost. Even the church was demolished and coffins dug up from the graveyard for burial at other parishes. Withnail brands Jake the poacher 'a silage heap' at the same spot, before declaring his intention of imminent stardom to nothing but a misty void. Jake was played by the croaky voiced Michael Elphick, a former friend of Robinson's from their time together at London's Central School of Speech and Drama and probably best known as the private investigator Ken Boon, from ITV's long running drama series in the late 1980s. Another essential place to visit on the Withnail pilgrimage is the iconic Gilbert Scott red phone box in the tiny village of Bampton, a few miles north of Shap.

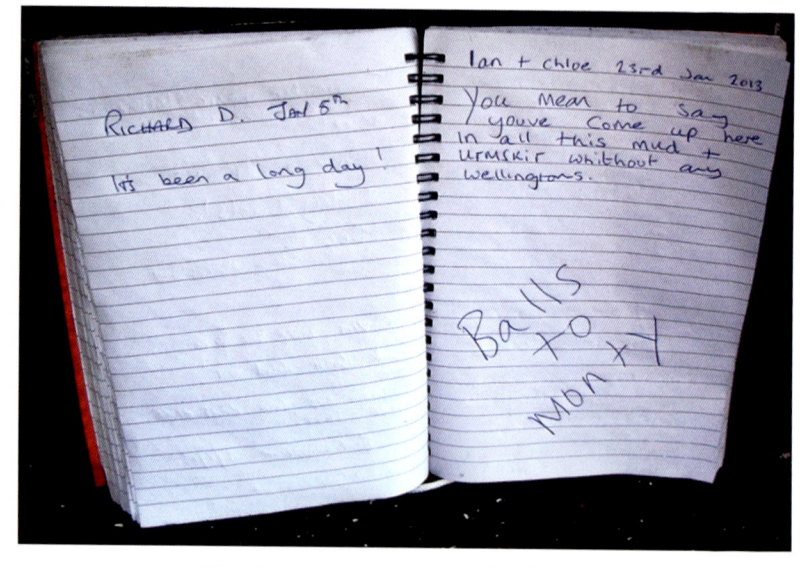

Classic quotes from the signing-in book.

There is even a signing-in book inside, where visitors can share their favourite quotes and mention websites related to the film. Withnail makes a heated call to his agent here, before turning down an offer to understudy the part of Konstantin in Russian playwright, Anton Chekov's play, *The Seagull*. The phone book even has what appears to be two shillings taped to its cover; a reference to the amount Withnail loses when it eats-up the last of his money.

The infamous bull scene where Marwood desperately throws his shopping in the air before charging foolhardily at an aroused bull was filmed just outside Bampton at Scarside Farm. Thankfully, for McGann, the animal had become frightened by the presence of a large film crew and ran away through the gate during filming. Mrs Parkin's farmhouse where he attempts to buy 'eggs and things' is located nearby at Tailbert, in the hamlet of Keld, a mile south-west of Shap.

There is no doubt British Telecom would risk a national outcry if they ever tried to sell off the Bampton phone box, which is now indisputably an iconic piece of film memorabilia. A number of fans on the *Withnail and I* forum website have even expressed an intention of turning it into a shrine, if it was ever put up for sale. In the future, perhaps Bampton will take over from Crow Crag, as the place where a legion of devotees will come to worship one of the most loved and endlessly quoted British films ever made.

Wet Sleddale reservoir near Shap, CA10 3NE. Grid ref: NY 55500 11400.
Haweswater reservoir, CA10 2RP. Grid ref: NY 48000 14000.
Bampton, CA10 2QR. Grid ref: NY 52164 18078.
For *Withnail and I* locations see frontispiece map.

Without a Clue Thom Eberhardt, 1988

'Meet the world's greatest detective… and Sherlock Holmes!'

Certificate: PG Colour: 107 minutes
Producers: Diana Buckhantz (associate), Ben Moses (associate), Marc Stirdivant
Screenplay: Gary Murphy, Larry Strawther Photography: Alan Hume
Music: Henry Mancini
Cast: Michael Caine, Ben Kingsley, Lysette Anthony, Peter Cook

Cinema's most filmed character, namely Sherlock Holmes leaves his famous Baker Street home behind to search for evidence in the Lake District during Thom Eberhardt's entertaining spoof comedy. Michael Caine is an out of work actor called Reginald Kincaid, hired by Dr. Watson to play the great detective. However, the most obvious clue is in the film's title, for it seems Holmes couldn't detect horse manure even if he stepped in it!

The film is a period Victorian farce, with Caine's fictional cockney Sherlock an egotistical, gambler and drunkard, constantly belittled by his creator Watson (Ben Kingsley). As the story unravels, their usual roles are completely reversed, as a broke, idiotic Holmes fumbles along painfully at times, relying on the real detective (Watson) to constantly prompt and bail him out. However, as Holmes' popularity with both senior figures of the establishment and public somehow soars, Watson becomes increasingly exasperated and jealous of the hammy Kincaid.

The seemingly effortless chemistry struck-up onscreen between Caine and Kingsley is a source of mild amusement, whilst they are ably supported

Sunrise over Windermere from Queen Adelaide's Hill.

by a stellar cast including: Jeffrey Jones (*Ferris Bueller's Day Off*) as a predictably sneering Inspector Lestrade, Nigel Davenport (*Chariots of Fire*) as a fittingly haughty Lord Smithwick and Paul Freeman (*Raiders of the Lost Ark*) as a villainous Professor Moriarty. The beautiful British actress Lysette Anthony plays a two-faced heroine Leslie Giles with the ineffable Peter Cook in a cameo role as Norman Greenhough, editor of the 'Strand' magazine, where Watson's accounts of the Sherlock Holmes stories appear. Ironically, Cook had played Sherlock some ten years earlier in a 1978 version of *The Hound of the Baskervilles*.

The case of the stolen Bank of England Plates is based around a series of forged five-pound notes. Watson is quickly on the trail when he finds a torn piece of paper with 'ermere' written on it. Receiving no input from a typically sozzled Holmes, he successfully deduces it should read 'Windermere' and must form part of a map where the chief suspect has travelled. Hastily, they decide to hotfoot it up to Cumbria, as the game is still afoot! They journey on a steam train, which terminates at the Lakeside station of the Haverthwaite railway at the southern end of Windermere. Now celebrating over 40 years in steam, this picturesque railway runs for three and a half miles along the banks of the River Leven, from the Haverthwaite to Lakeside stations. Passengers can then alight and board one of the steamers bound for Bowness or Ambleside, combined with a visit to the Lakes Aquarium, Motor Museum or World of Beatrix Potter attractions.

At the Lakeside pier Holmes and Watson are given a rapturous welcome by a gathering of local dignitaries and members of the general public. They are then driven in a horse-drawn carriage along Derwent Hill in Portinscale (near

Keswick) to their hotel, one of Miss Potter's former favourites, Fawe Park.

The following morning they meet the mayor at a cottage rented by Leslie Giles' father Peter, beside Windermere's eastern shore. Here they make a gruesome discovery when an innocent man named Donald Ayres is pulled out of the cold, black looking water. This scene was filmed at Millerground Boathouse, a popular place with walkers that affords the best access to the lake from the car park at Rayrigg Road. Beside the boathouse at Low Millerground, is a seventeenth century cottage with a bell tower (minus the bell now) that used to be sounded to summon the ferryman. In the past a rowing boat foot ferry used to cross Windermere over to Belle Grange. If you investigate closely on the path out to Rayrigg Hall, you will discover a large rock at the water's edge with a plaque attached, marking the spot where King William IV's wife, Adelaide came ashore in 1840 on a visit to Windermere. Back at the car park on Rayrigg Road, there is a kissing-gate with a well-worn track leading gently upwards to Queen Adelaide Hill, one of seven former 'viewing stations' dotted around Windermere, famously designated by Thomas West in his guidebook to the Lake District in 1778.

During the eighteenth century the supposed 'savage grandeur' of the region gave way to the emergence of the picturesque movement, as a fashion for perceiving landscape from certain viewpoints, became popular with both tourists and artists alike. Claife Station, now a grade II listed ruin, was another such station situated on Windermere's western shore. The National Trust now owns both of these viewpoints. During Claife's heyday, visitors would have actually turned their back on the landscape to hold up a 'Claude glass' (named after the French landscape painter Claude Lorrain 1600-82), presenting them with an especially framed view seen through different coloured glass.

Queen Adelaide's Hill, LA 23 1BP. Grid ref: SD 40300 98400.
Portinscale, Keswick, CA12 5RN. Grid ref: NY 24922 23620.
The Lakeside & Haverthwaite Railway, LA12 8AL. Grid ref: SD 34958 84247.

Selected Cumbrian Cinemas

Alhambra – Keswick and Penrith

A visit to the Lake District would not be complete without going to see a screening at the Keswick Alhambra. Why? Well, they've been entertaining audiences for 100 years for one thing. Add to that an ornate Edwardian facade decorating a two-storey building, traditional stalls and a balcony with decorative bands across a flattened barrel vault ceiling. However, despite these wonderful surroundings, the cinema has often been threatened with closure. Recently though, it has fared much better with new seats for 246 people and the installation of Dolby Digital Sound.

The cinema still has a 35mm film projector in order to screen classic films. It is also the home of the Keswick Film club, who meet every Sunday evening from September to March. The club was formed in December 1999, and produced its first short season of ten films between February and April of the same year. It is run by a group of film enthusiasts who aim to bring the best thought-provoking films from both British and World cinema to local people

Alhambra Cinema, Keswick.

and the surrounding area, who are often not able to see high quality independent films in the more mainstream cinemas.

The Lonsdale Alhambra Penrith is located in the heart of the town and provides a first-class cinema experience, screening all the latest cinema releases as well as independent and foreign-language films in comfortable and relaxing surroundings. The cinema, like its Keswick counterpart, is now fully equipped with Dolby Digital projection and Dolby Digital sound. Darren Horne, a former manager also produced the cult 2010 film *The Maniac Project*, which was screened there in 2012.

Fellinis/Zefirellis – Ambleside

Named after the former Italian director and screenwriter Federico Fellini (1920-93) who was one of the most influential filmmakers of the twentieth century, Fellinis aim to show the latest studio movies and art-house films in a unique cinema experience situated in the central Lake District. Occasionally more recent Hollywood releases are screened in its new state of the art digital format. Audiences can enjoy a range of chilled wines and cold beers in a cinematic experience based solely on comfort. From time to time, the cinema also broadcasts live performances of popular shows from the world of opera, theatre, art and ballet via satellite whilst the exterior and front doors of Fellinis featured as a location in David Thewlis's unreleased film *Cheeky* in 2003.

The enduringly popular independent cinema Zefirellis (named after another Italian director, Franco Zefirelli) is situated close to Fellinis in Ambleside. It became known in the early 1980s as a cinema and restaurant, when it displayed older former projection equipment from the 1920s in the foyer. The Windermere & Ambleside Cinema Co. Ltd. ran the cinema until the 1950s, when a group known as M.B.C. Cinemas Ltd. took control. During the 1960s it became an Arts Centre as well as a large cinema with some 350 seats. Nowadays they offer a mainstream weekly programme, but always with the aim of supporting new and emerging talents within the world of cinema and the arts. The cinema boasts five decent sized screens all furnished with state of the art Dolby Digital technology, air conditioning and induction loops, plus Screens 1 and 3 have Dolby 3D capability.

The Roxy – Ulverston

Having recently celebrated its 75th year, the 1930s traditional family Art-deco auditorium has all its original features still intact with over 300 seats and one of the largest cinema-scope screens in Cumbria. It also puts on a diverse programme of recent and classic arty flicks on the second Thursday of every month as part of the Roxy Film Club (which has been running for over 25 years). In the 1970s the building was split into a cinema/bingo operation, with the cinema occupying the original circle. In the late 1990s it was dealt a potential blow when the six-screen Apollo cinema opened in nearby Barrow-in-Furness. Since September 2006 the Northern Morris Cinema chain has leased the cinema, with the bingo operation ceasing to exist in 2007.

The Royalty - Bowness-on-Windermere

The former public hall originally opened in 1926 after being built by public subscription. It had been designed to provide cinema, theatre and dance facilities. These days it is a three-screen cinema owned by Northern Morris Cinemas with Digital projection and Dolby Stereo sound. The main screen retains the original auditorium and its 1930s ambience with 400 seats in stalls and circle. Screen 2 is a self-contained cinema with 100 seats, whilst screen 3 is a studio cinema with 65 seats. 3D films are also shown.

What makes the Royalty Cinema unique is a rare Wurlitzer Theatre Pipe Organ dating from 1927. It originally belonged to an American Theatre in Cleveland, Ohio until 1934, before it made the long journey across the Atlantic Ocean to be installed in the Rex Cinema in Stratford, East London. There it remained until the early 1970s when it was removed and put into storage. The Furness Theatre Organ Project acquired the instrument and began a painstaking restoration in spring 2007. On completion, the first concert with the rejuvenated organ was held at the Royalty in October 2012. Concerts are now held monthly between spring and autumn, with special events at other times.

Film Festivals

Keswick – 'The Friendly Film Festival'
(held every February/March)

Movie buff Tony Martin used the experience he gained from running an award winning film club in Wales to even greater effect when he moved up to Keswick in the late 1990s. Once settled, he founded a film festival in 2000, after setting up a club the previous year. The idea was to have especially themed festivals showcasing films from all over the world, whilst promoting children's and family features alongside 'shorts' made by local filmmakers. Now firmly established, the festival has become renowned as Cumbria's premiere film event, bringing new, recent and overlooked releases to the Lake District.

The self-styled 'friendly film festival' now boasts a legendary Hollywood actor as its patron, namely John Hurt (*Alien, The Elephant Man, Tinker Tailor Soldier Spy*) who attended for the first time in 2012. Held in late February, its varied programme is one of the main cultural attractions in the pretty market town, with screenings taking place at the Theatre by the Lake (just a stone's throw from the beautiful shores of Derwentwater), the 100-year-old

A packed audience for 'Radiator' at the Theatre by the Lake, 2015,
© Keswick Film Festival.

Alhambra Cinema and massive IMAX screen at the Rheged centre, on the outskirts of Penrith.

Festivalgoers are also regularly treated to informative question and answer sessions from directors and cast members, whilst the annual Osprey Short Film Awards showcase new films with a Cumbrian connection.

Kendal Mountain Festival
(held every November)
Since beginning in 1999, the festival has developed into an international event attracting film premieres from around the globe. During four action-packed days every November, one of the world's leading mountain film festivals sets out to inspire more people to explore, enjoy and represent mountains, wilderness and their cultures. The main focus of the festival programme is the 'mountain film competition' that normally screens over 50 films (picked from around 200 or so entries) with ten sought after prizes to be won. Films are usually screened at the Brewery Arts Centre, which began to show 35mm films in the late 1980s, until a larger cinema of 276 seats opened within the same complex.

Visitors can expect to see films from plenty of other genres too, ranging from: culture, drama, wildlife and environmental documentaries alongside a huge lecture programme. Amongst other festival highlights are numerous arts and literature events, plus the 'Adventure Film Academy' for up and coming filmmakers, which involves the BBC and other leading organisations. The festival claims to boost the local economy to the tune of some £1.5 million each year, whilst *The Sunday Times* has famously referred to it as one of the main reasons young people are drawn to live in Kendal.

Picnic Cinema
(events held throughout the summer)
Films with a Cumbrian connection are nearly always on the menu for the outdoor film-screening programme organised by Eden Arts. The agency has become responsible for arts happenings ranging from open studios to sculpture in trees. All profits go to a good cause, including Eden Art's rural touring cinema programme, 'Remote', which brings free cinema equipment to rural villages.

Over recent years, Picnic Cinema's quirky usherettes and strange projectionists have rolled out a monster line-up of movies to remote locations in Cumbria, Yorkshire, Lancashire and County Durham. Film lovers have been able to choose from one-off screenings in forest sites or themed camp-over events held at unique venues, including the romantic Lowther Castle and suitably haunted Muncaster Castle.

'It's just the maddest idea, taking our huge cinema screen, plonking it down in the middle of a forest or an extraordinary Gothic castle and screening classic films,' says Adrian Lochhead, Eden Arts Director. 'I think everyone realises that it's something special, an opportunity to do something that is really out of the ordinary.' In collaboration with the Forestry Commission, the series of films has included Danny Boyle's marauding zombies in *28 Days Later,* shown at both Hamsterley near Bishop Auckland and Grizedale Forest, with Ben Wheatley's black comedy *Sightseers* reaching new levels of creepiness when it was screened at Keswick's Pencil Museum in 2013.

Pre-entertainment in the courtyard of Crow Crag at a 'Withnail and I' screening, © 2012, Eden Arts.

Since 2012, fans of the cult classic *Withnail and I* have been able to pay homage to their heroes during annual pilgrimages to Uncle Monty's cottage, Crow Crag. With an emphasis on fun, Eden Arts always urge picnickers to go in costume. 'Dressing up is very much encouraged at all the cinema events. Audience members get unique access to castles after dark, to see films where they were made and experience great drives on forest roads that are not normally accessible to members of the public,' says Project Manager Heather Walker. And if you ever decide to dust down your tent and take in a movie under the stars, don't forget their motto, 'Pack wisely, picnickers!'

Western Lakes Film Festival, Whitehaven
(held every June)
Organised by the Whitehaven Festival Company (founded in 1998 and run by volunteers ever since), the inaugural Film Festival took place over the weekend of 19 and 20 June 2015. An impressive and wide-ranging line-up of films ran continuously across a number of venues. There was also a continental market with over 160 stalls, a special 'Cars of the Stars' exhibition

displaying *Ghostbusters'* Ecto 1 and the Adam West Batmobile, as well as airshows from The Red Arrows and Battle of Britain re-enactors.

Pop-up cinema screens were installed at the Queen's Dock car park, Bulwark Quay, Harbour Promenade, along with the Vault Store at the Rum Story Museum. A standout feature of the festival encompassed a special re-opening of the mothballed Gaiety Cinema (formerly opened in 1922 and closed since August 2003). Some of the film highlights included classics such as: *The Dambusters, The Great Escape, Casablanca and Breakfast At Tiffany's* shown alongside children's favourites *E.T., The Lego Movie* and *The Lion King*. Several cult classics were screened, ranging from *The Dark Knight Trilogy, The Rocky Horror Picture Show* and *The Commitments* (where the film was followed by a concert from members of the original cast).

However, the festival made international headlines for almost disastrous reasons, after a Red Devil skydiver had to be saved by a teammate after his parachute failed to open in mid-air. The chute had become tangled at around 18,000 feet above the ground, but thanks to some quick thinking, the pair eventually landed safely into the water at Queen's Dock. The dramatic escape was watched by thousands of visitors who immediately took to social media to share videos and describe their shock and admiration for the team. Their spectacular exploits were even honoured by a pie shop in Whitehaven who renamed its steak and ale pie, The Red Devil!

Websites
for more information on selected locations:

Across the Lake
Coniston Sun Hotel: www.thesunconiston.com
The Ruskin Museum: www.ruskinmuseum.com
Fell and Rock Climbing Club: www.frcc.co.uk
Alien Blood
Hay Bridge Nature Reserve: www.haybridgereserve.org.uk
Century on the Crags
http://www.stridingedge.com/index.html
Cheeky
Kurt Schwitters: http://www.littoral.org.uk/merzbarn.html
Cloud Cuckoo Land
Upfront Gallery, Penrith: http://www.up-front.com
The Clouded Yellow
http://www.golakes.co.uk/grasmere-and-rydal/
http://www.nationaltrust.org.uk/aira-force-and-ullswater/
The Dambusters:
http://www.langdalechase.co.uk
The Darkest Light:
Ribblehead Viaduct: http://www.visitcumbria.com/carlset/ribblehead-viaduct/
Malham Cove: http://www.malhamdale.com/cove.htm
Deep Lies
Lodore Falls Hotel: http://www.lakedistricthotels.net/lodorefalls/index.php
Castlerigg stone circle: http://www.english-heritage.org.uk/visit/places/castlerigg-stone-circle/
Downhill
Honister Slate Mine: http://www.honister.com
The Wainwright Society: http://www.wainwright.org.uk/coasttocoast.html
The French Lieutenant's Woman
Windermere Motor Boat Racing Club: http://www.wmbrc.co.uk
Blackwell, Bowness-on-Windermere: https://www.blackwell.org.uk
The Gentle Sex
Carlisle Castle: http://www.english-heritage.org.uk/visit/places/carlisle-castle/
If Only
Honister Crag: http://www.honister.com
Julia
Keswick Country House Hotel: http://www.thekeswickhotel.co.uk
Killer's Moon
Armathwaite Hall Hotel: http://www.armathwaite-hall.com

AN A TO Z: CUMBRIA AND THE LAKE DISTRICT ON FILM

Lakeland Rock
Striding Edge: http://www.stridingedge.com
Life of a Mountain: Scafell Pike
Terry Abraham: http://www.terryabrahamlakedistrictvideo.wordpress.com
Striding Edge: http://www.stridingedge.com
Wasdale Head Show and Shepherds Meet: http://www.wasdaleheadshow.co.uk
The Maniac Project
Penrith Cinema: http://www.penrith-alhambra.co.uk
Miss Potter
Hill Top: http://www.nationaltrust.org.uk/hill-top/
Beatrix Potter Gallery:
    http://www.nationaltrust.org.uk/beatrix-potter-gallery-and-hawkshead/
The Rum Story, Whitehaven: http://www.rumstory.co.uk
Noble
Christina Noble Children's Foundation: https://www.cncf.org
The Dock Museum, Barrow: www.dockmuseum.org.uk
The One That Got Away
Grizedale Forest: http://www.forestry.gov.uk/grizedale
Pandaemonium
Wordsworth Trust: https://www.wordsworth.org.uk/home.html
Friends of Coleridge: http://www.friendsofcoleridge.com
The Paradine Case
Langdale Chase Hotel, Windermere: http://www.langdalechase.co.uk
Drunken Duck Inn, Barngates: http://drunkenduckinn.co.uk
Yew Tree Farm, Coniston: http://www.yewtree-farm.com
The Pike
Low Wood Sports Centre, Windermere: http://englishlakes.co.uk/watersports/
Postman Pat: The Movie
Brewery Arts Centre, Kendal: https://www.breweryarts.co.uk
The Raven on the Jetty
Rheged Centre: http://www.rheged.com
She'll be Wearing Pink Pyjamas
Eskdale Outward Bound Centre: http://www.outwardbound.org.uk/centres/eskdale/
Sightseers
The Pencil Museum, Keswick: http://www.pencilmuseum.co.uk
Park Cliffe campsite, Windermere: http://www.parkcliffe.co.uk
Snow White and the Huntsman
Three Shires Inn (for Cathedral Cave):
    http://www.visitcumbria.com/amb/cathedral-cave/
Soft Top Hard Shoulder
Lancaster Services: http://www.motorwayservices.info/lancaster_forton_services_m6
Soldiers of the Damned
Greystoke: http://www.greystoke.com
Swallows and Amazons
Arthur Ransome Trust: http://www.arthur-ransome-trust.org.uk

Museum of Lakeland Life: https://www.lakelandmuseum.org.uk
Bank Ground Farm: http://www.bankground.com
Platty Plus: http://www.plattyplus.co.uk
Three and Out
Ruskin Museum: http://www.ruskinmuseum.com
Black Bull, Coniston: http://www.blackbullconiston.co.uk
27 Memory Lane
Farfield Mill: http://www.farfieldmill.org
28 Days Later
Ennerdale: http://www.wildennerdale.co.uk
We're Here For A Good Time, Not A Long Time
Keswick Launch Company: http://www.keswick-launch.co.uk
Dalebottom Farm: http://www.dalebottomfarm.co.uk/about.htm
Watch the film: https://vimeo.com/125122060
Withnail and I
Withnail and I Forum: http://withnailandiforum.com
Celebrate: LGBT History in Cumbria: http://www.celebratecumbria.co.uk
Without a Clue
The Lakeside & Haverthwaite Railway: http://www.lakesiderailway.co.uk

Selected Cumbrian Cinemas
Alhambra, Keswick: http://www.keswick-alhambra.co.uk/
Alhambra, Penrith: http://www.penrith-alhambra.co.uk/
Fellinis, Ambleside: http://www.fellinisambleside.com/cinema
Zeffirellis, Ambleside: http://www.zeffirellis.com/
The Roxy, Ulverston: http://ulverston.nm-cinemas.co.uk/
The Royalty, Bowness-on-Windermere: http://windermere.nm-cinemas.co.uk/

Cumbrian Film Festivals
Keswick Film Festival: http://www.keswickfilmclub.org/kff/
Kendal Mountain Festival: http://www.mountainfest.co.uk/
Picnic Cinema: http://www.edenarts.co.uk/portfolio/picnic-cinema/
Western Lakes Film Festival, Whitehaven: http://www.westernlakesfilmfestival.org.uk

Afterword

On Thursday, 17 December 2015, the most hugely anticipated film of all time finally landed at cinema screens across the UK. *Star Wars Episode VII: The Force Awakens* opened to a host of five star reviews and rapidly went on to smash box office records worldwide. The power of the Force certainly prompted many local cinemas in Cumbria to fully embrace the sense of occasion. At the Royalty in Bowness-on-Windermere, a handful of Stormtroopers were even drafted in to sell popcorn and ice creams on the opening night.

The film now stands at number two on the all-time highest grossing list nestled in behind James Cameron's all conquering *Avatar*. With a nostalgic nod to the earlier films, J. J. Abrams skilfully re-established the Star Wars franchise for old and new fans alike. The fantastic shot of the X-Wings of the Resistance skimming across the surface of Derwentwater has also given the Lake District one of its most iconic film sequences to date. The Royal Mail acknowledged this by putting the same image on the cover of an exclusive book of Star Wars stamps printed especially to commemorate the film's release. Whilst a couple of teaser trailers similarly featured the spaceships exhibiting typical derring-do low flying over Thirlmere in the shadow of the mighty Raven Crag.

According to Creative England, 2016 is already shaping up to be a bumper year for both film and TV in the North West. With acclaimed projects like ITV's *Safe House* returning to film another series at Coniston. There is even the mouth-watering prospect of J. K. Rowling's latest detective novel *Career of Evil* filming in Barrow, where three of its chapters were set. One of the only blots on the filmic landscape remains the absence of 007 from England's largest national park. But surely it is only a matter of time before James Bond locks horns (and wheels) on the hairpin bends of a Lakeland mountain pass.

Undoubtedly, another hugely anticipated release to look forward to will be the BBC & Harbour films new adaptation of *Swallows and Amazons*. Like Claude Whatham's charming original 1974 film, scenes filmed in the Lake District at Coniston and Derwentwater (during June/July 2015) will naturally play a starring role. With such a high profile release returning to show off the area's magic once again, the onscreen future certainly looks bright for Cumbria and the Lake District.

Here's to a future where the hills are once again, alive with sounds of playback…

Acknowledgements

I would like to express my sincerest thanks to the following people for all their help and advice throughout the last couple of years: Dawn Robertson and the team at Hayloft, Terry Abraham, Mark Blaney at Footprint Films and Christine Llewellyn-Reeve, Ellen Bowness, Tom Browne at Turnchapel Films, The Carnforth Centre, Jon Clifford at Timeless Films, Ryan Driscoll, Andrew Elliott and Darren Horne, Tim Ellis, Lizzie Goodman at Crisis Films, Kerry Harrison, Luke Hupton at Lupton Films, Janet Knudsen at One Day Films, LeeAnn Lennox at Armathwaite Hall, Robbie Moffat at Palmtree Films, Stephen Rigg at Blackdog Productions, Thorney How Independent Hostel – Grasmere, Vicky Slowe at the Ruskin Museum, Peter White at WMBRC, David and Angie Unsworth, Gill Cowton, Tim 'The Pike' Balchin and everyone at the Heaton Cooper Studio, Grasmere, Dr. William Smith, Iain 'I don't believe it' Sharpe, Massimo Moretti at Studio Canal, Jonathan at Alamy, Eden Arts, Sharron Drake at Lucasfilm, Daniel Hochard at Imagex Fonts and Nina Claridge for her kind permission to use a photograph on the cover.

Finally, special thanks to Paul McGeoch for the jacket design and to Eileen Pun for her wonderful map drawings and continual encouragement. Notwithstanding the extremely gracious Sophie Neville for her time, advice and invaluable information.

Film Index

A
Across the Lake	19
Alien Blood	21
Axed	23

B
B. Monkey	26
Bollywood (Lamhe, Mujhse Dosti Karoge, Mr Bhatti on Chutti, Nammanna)	28
Brazil	31
Brief Encounter	33

C
Century on the Crags	38
Cheeky	40
Cloud Cuckoo Land	42
The Clouded Yellow	45

D
The Dambusters	48
The Darkest Light	50
Deep Lies	53
Downhill	54

F
The French Lieutenant's Woman	57

G
The Gentle Sex	60

I
If Only	62

J
Julia	64

K
Ken Russell's Films (Gothic, Mahler, The Rainbow, Tommy)	66
Killer's Moon	71
Killing Me Softly	73

L
- Lakeland Rock — 76
- Let Sleeping Corpses Lie — 78
- Life of a Mountain: Scafell Pike — 79
- The Loss of Sexual Innocence

M
- The Maniac Project — 83
- Miss Potter — 87

N
- No Blade of Grass — 94
- Noble — 97

O
- The One That Got Away — 100

P
- Pandaemonium — 103
- The Paradine Case — 106
- The Pike — 109
- The Plague Dogs — 110
- Postman Pat — 112

R
- Radiator — 115
- The Raven on the Jetty — 119

S
- She'll Be Wearing Pink Pyjamas — 122
- Sightseers — 124
- Snow White and the Huntsman — 127
- Soft Top Hard Shoulder — 129
- Soldiers of the Damned — 131
- Star Wars Episode VII: The Force Awakens — 134
- The Stars Look Down — 136
- Swallows and Amazons — 138

T
- Three and Out — 147
- 27 Memory Lane — 149
- 28 Days Later — 151

W
- We're Here For A Good Time, Not A Long Time — 153
- Withnail and I — 155
- Without a Clue — 161

The author

David has spent the last ten years or so at some of the most prestigious museums and galleries in both London and Cumbria, whilst working in the Music Industry before then. He graduated from Goldsmiths College, University of London with a BA in History of Art, and still hopes to complete a Masters degree in Lake District Landscape studies at Lancaster University.

When he is not writing or watching films he can usually be found daydreaming on a hill somewhere…

His website address is: www.filmsmadeincumbria.com
and Twitter name: @theArtBagger